BRADFORD-ON-AVON MUSEUM MONOGRAPH No. 4

BRADFORD-ON-AVON PROBATE INVENTORIES

1550-1700

Ivor Slocombe

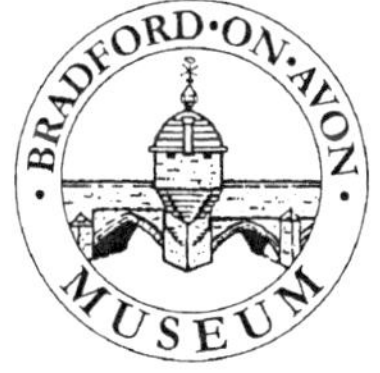

In association with Ex Libris Press

Published in 2021 by
Bradford on Avon Museum

www.bradfordonavonmuseum.co.uk

in association with Ex Libris Press

Origination by Ex Libris Press
www.ex-librisbooks.co.uk

Printed by TPM Ltd.,
Farrington Gurney, Somerset

ISBN 978-1-912020-12-6

CONTENTS

TRADES

Introduction

An Act of 1529 required the executors of a will to appoint 'two honest persons to make or cause to be made a trewe and perfyte inventory of all the goodes, catells, wares, merchaundyses as well as movable as not movable whatsoever'. One copy of the inventory was to be retained by the executors and the other deposited with the Bishop's commissioners. The main object of this was to provide the information which would allow anyone to check whether the terms of the will had been properly carried out.

Although this requirement was introduced in 1529, the first extant Bradford-on-Avon inventory is that of Richard Colborne in 1552. The inventories become more frequent after 1570 but the bulk are from the 17th century. This collection comprises 89 inventories; there are a few others from this period but they have not been included as being too little in content or the original document is too damaged to be usable. They cover a wide range of people and occupations. Firstly a number of yeomen and husbandmen then, as might be expected, those connected with the cloth industry from clothiers to clothworkers, weavers and fullers. A range of other trades is represented including blacksmiths, bakers, inn holders and glovers. Finally there are a number of females, usually widows.

These probate inventories are exceptionally valuable to the historian as they give an excellent social and economic picture of the period. In particular, it was the practice of the examiners to go around the house and to record what was in each room. This allows us to reconstruct the house itself together with the use of each room. It highlights the differences between the variety of trades from the most wealthy with quite large houses and a wide range of possessions to the more lowly with a quite basic house and relatively little furniture and other goods. The inventories also provide us with details of the working tools and other items connected to the various trades and, for the husbandman, a good picture of the type of agriculture being practised in the area. Finally, most inventories have an item which values and sometimes gives details of the dead person's wearing apparel.

The houses

The basic house consisted of two rooms on the ground floor, a hall and a kitchen, with two chambers above. The old medieval hall open to the rafters had disappeared by this time with a chamber over the hall being most common. Also, at least by the 17th century, most of the houses detailed in these inventories seemed to have expanded with more rooms on the ground floor and subsequently an equivalent number of chambers above. Butteries appear as well as the kitchen and various lofts start to be mentioned, especially the cheese loft and occasionally the malt loft. In a few instances a cellar is mentioned but this seems to have been a room on the ground floor rather than underground. Perhaps the most notable of the developments was the appearance of the parlour, sometimes an additional room being built on but more usually, a room created by dividing off part of the hall. For some trades the shop or workshop forms part of the house. Outside, especially with the husbandmen, there could be a range of buildings such as the white house or dairy and a malt house.

The rooms

The hall was very much a multi-purpose room. It was usually furnished with a table (a 'table board') and with stools and forms rather than chairs. The invariable presence of 'hangells, spits, pothooks, andirons and brandirons, iron dogs, fire pans, tongs and bellows indicate that there must have been a large fireplace which was also used for cooking. Wooden plates and trenchers occur but pewter (and iron for cooking vessels) was the most common metal with, occasionally, bell metal. But brass, used for pans, was clearly the most valuable and the most prized. Pewter or brass candlesticks are frequently recorded.

The kitchen usually had a range of plates, bowls and cooking utensils as in the hall. But we also very commonly find sieves, basting ladles, skimmers and warming pans. In the larger houses, the more elaborate food preparations are indicated by the presence of spice mortars.

The buttery , as well as having kitchen stores, often had a range of brewing equipment including malt sieves, troughs for steeping barley for making malt, and sometimes a separate furnace.

The 'new' parlour tended to be more comfortably furnished. Apart from the usual table and forms, it might have leather chairs, a cupboard and some floor coverings. In some cases it was also being used as a bedroom with bedsteads, cushions, curtains and wall hangings.

In the chambers or bedrooms the inventories describe various types of bedstead. The most elaborate was the tester bedstead together with a half-headed bedstead and a standing bedstead. On the bedstead would be a flock bed (cloth case filled with waste wool) or more expensively a feather bed. In addition were pillows, bolsters, coverlets and blankets . The finest sheets were made of holland cloth but one also finds canvas sheets made from a coarse cloth. Depending on the wealth of the owner, the rooms might be furnished with chests, coffers, chairs and sometimes a table. Some were really very comfortable with rugs, curtains and, in two cases, with looking glasses. With only a small number of chambers, it was not uncommon to find several beds in each room. Also there were truckle beds which, when not in use, would push under the main bed. Particularly with the husbandmen, the chambers might also be used to store farm tools, bags of wool and bushels of malt.

The lofts might have some bedsteads (perhaps for servants) but they were mainly used for such things as cheeses and the equipment for making cheese. Again one might find there a whole range of tools, old chests and other unwanted equipment.

The most common of the outside buildings was the white house. There we find the dairy utensils such as churns, pails and tubs, but, most importantly, the equipment for cheese making such as the cheese presses and vats.

Wearing apparel and other personal possessions

Most inventories give the value of the dead person's clothing. This tended to range from about £1 up to £10 for the wealthier yeomen. The fact they often left particular items of clothing in their wills to various people, also indicates that clothes were expensive and highly prized. For the men, details of the clothes are seldom mentioned but they are in the case of Henry Bapshin, a husbandman. He had two coats, a doublet, two pairs of hose, a cloak and two hats. Robert Phipp, a vintner, had two hats, three jerkins, three doublets, four pairs of breeches, one cloak, six shirts and three night caps all worth £5. The items of clothing of the females are much more usually listed. Elizabeth Howell, for example, had gowns, smocks, partlets, petticoats and aprons with the total value of £4 2s 6d.

Few other personal possessions are mentioned although some of the females had silver rings and a few had silver or silver gilt cups and spoons. Several people had a 'Bible and other books'.

Trades: tools and implements

A lot of information can be gleaned about the different trades and their tools.

Cloth industry. The dominance of the cloth industry is shown by the fact that 25, over a quarter, of these inventories are of men working in that industry – one clothier, five fullers, 3 clothworkers, 14 weavers, one worsted comber and one card maker. John Smith, one of the greatest of the clothiers, left possessions worth £677 of which £150 was the value of the lease on his property. Of the rest of his property, £442 represented the large amount of cloth that he owned. Robert Dicke and Anthony Matthew are good examples of clothworkers whose job it was to 'finish' the cloth. Both had a large number of shears together with shear boards, dubbing boards and presses. The broadweavers, as expected, had usually one or two broad looms but some also had quilting turns while John Davis was unusual in having two kersey looms. The inventory for John Smith, the wealthy clothier, particularly notes his white sorting cloths with his own red and green mark and his 15 cloths with a yellow copper mark. It is traditionally said that the weavers had their looms on the top floor of the house in order to get as much light as possible but this was not necessarily so. In these inventories there are seven cases where looms are mentioned and it is possible to identify their location. In five cases, the looms are in a separate workshop on the ground floor or in a separate room. In the other two cases, one is in the hall and the other in a lower chamber.

Mercers. If the clothiers were responsible for producing cloth, it was the mercers who were the great retailers and many were even more wealthy. William Audley's possessions were valued at £98 but it was Michael Tidcombe who outdid everyone with possessions worth £604. Their lifestyle reflected this wealth with each having silver spoons, dishes and bowls. They both had on offer a huge range of different sorts of cloth ranging from the very fine holland to the coarser fustian and canvas. Some of these were imported from the Low Countries and Germany. Interestingly they were also selling some, for the time, rather exotic goods – currants, raisins, metheglin, oil, honey, tobacco and vinegar.

Chandler. Henry Elliot, a chandler, also illustrates the very wide range of luxury goods which were available in the late 17th century. Apart from candles and tallow, he offered such things as molasses, sugar and spices. He also sold tobacco which he seems to have processed himself from raw, leaf tobacco.

Most intriguing is the reference to 'growings' which suggests he had access to locally grown tobacco. This was highly illegal and the Crown, through the local magistrates, made intense efforts to discover and destroy this illicit crop.

Coopers, blacksmiths and carpenters. With ale being the common drink of all classes of society, brewing both commercial and home, was extremely important and hence also the role of the cooper, the maker of barrels. John Orpen was obviously running a huge business. His stock was worth £60 and included hundreds if not thousands of wooden 'staves' and other timber used in making his range of barrels from hogsheads to the smaller kilderkins. The process of blacksmithing was probably little different from that of today. The inventories of William Howell and James Watts list the very familiar tools of their trade – anvils, bellows, vices, pincers, files and hammers – as well as a stock of iron bars and old iron for 'recycling'. The list of possessions of Henry Painter, a carpenter, is also particularly valuable for giving his tools in some details including axes, spokeshaves, planes, squares and hammers.

There is one **tanner**, Robert Whatly, with his own tanning pit and a stock of various sorts of hides including calf skins.

Of the other trades, perhaps the most interesting is Jasper Drewett, a **wire drawer**. He had a bundle of wire, some old working tools and benches while in the kitchen he had two wire candlesticks most likely of his own making.

Innholders

Two innholders are included – Robert Townsend in 1630 and Edward Dick in 1668 – but it is not certain which inns they held. Townsend certainly had quite a large establishment. Apart from a beer cellar with several hogsheads of beer, he also had a quantity of wine including sack, claret and white wine. The inn had six bedchambers and a significant amount of bed linen showing that he was providing accommodation as well as refreshment. Edward Dick seems to have had a smaller inn serving just beer and, having just two bedchambers, there was only very limited accommodation if at all.

Agriculture

There are inventories for 12 yeomen and 15 husbandmen all engaged in agriculture. The difference between a yeoman and a husbandman was essentially a matter of status with the yeoman ranking just below the gentry while the husbandman was just a farmer. The yeoman was more likely to hold his land freehold rather than leasehold or copyhold but this was changing quite quickly. In general, also, the yeomen were more prosperous. The average value of the possessions of the Bradford yeomen was £166 compared with £67 for the husbandmen. But there was considerable overlap. Edmund Parker (£183), John Barton (£157) and Thomas Kelson (£152), husbandmen. were more wealthy than some who called themselves yeomen.

The main agricultural areas, apart from Barton Farm, were at Trowle and Widbrook to the south of the town and Cumberwell. Woolley and Bradford Leigh to the north. The farming was mixed with all having both livestock and arable. Sheep predominated for just a few – John Barton with 100 sheep at Widbrook, Thomas Black with 90 sheep and lambs and John Bailey with 50. Other livestock included cows, pigs and poultry. Cheese was clearly one of the most important products and many had flitches of bacon hanging in their kitchen. There were surprisingly few horses and the reference to saddles, bridles and pack saddles suggest they were mostly used for personal riding or carrying goods. Oxen were much more common and these were obviously used for ploughing. The inventories list a whole range of plough implements including ploughs, harrows and plough harness. The arable crops were wheat, oats, pease and vetches. Barley was grown to produce malt which was processed and used to brew beer on the farm. Ale was made without hops which was the normal practice but Henry Painter, a carpenter, seems to have brewed beer having a 'frail' with hops in it. There are two mentions of bees – owned by John Hendy, a husbandman, and Henry Painter.

A number of artisans, such as weavers, still maintained some link with agriculture, having farming land and cattle. Luke Stevens, a weaver, had three cows, five sheep, two pigs and poultry as well as some wheat and barley. Thomas Hunt, a mason, had an even more substantial farming interest with 49 sheep.

Females

Any property a married woman might have was legally owned by her husband. So the females recorded here are widows or spinsters and many were relatively wealthy. Many of them seem to have carried on their husband's business usually in farming. The exception is Ann Box who is described as a widow and weaver. She had two broadlooms and other weaving equipment. Of the farmers, Elizabeth Taunton was the largest with possessions worth £118. She had oxen, cattle, pigs, and a range of ploughing equipment together with a store of corn and hay. Her personal possessions included silver salt cellars and spoons. Both Elizabeth Bapshin and Elizabeth Howell had mixed farms growing wheat and barley as well as keeping cattle. Both were engaged in cheese and butter making.

Other items

A number of the men had guns used for shooting game. John Moxham, a blacksmith, had a 'birding piece' and John Geatly, a yeoman, a 'fouling piece'. Some others had more offensive weapons – the muskets of John Bailey and John Moxham and the sword and two daggers of William Raynoldes. They were probably holding these as part of the requirement of the local militia.

There is just one reference to the Civil War which was raging for a significant part of this period. John Doggett, a weaver who died in 1643, was said to leave no wearing apparel because 'all his wearing apparel with divers linen and woollen was carried away by the King's army'.

Finally there is the nice little domestic touch with Christian Phillips whose possessions included one mouse snare.

A true Indentory

of all suche goode & challes
Moveable & unmoveable of Willm ffisher of Bradford
[...] in the county of wilte weaver, deceased
valued & praysed by Thomas ffisher Richard Donkin
and Thomas Rawlinge the xije of May, 1603

The Hall

In primis j Table borde & ij formes — xvjd
Item j Coffer & ij bowles — vjd
Item j Barrell & j payle — viijd
Item j old vate ij stooles j spynnyng whome & j rayne — xxviijd
Item j brasse croke j kettle j postnett & j skymmer — vs
Item j dossen of trenchers halfe a dossen of spones vj dishes & a ladle — viijd
Item j brode loome with all his furnitur — xs

The Chamber

Item j bordon bedstood with a florke bed ij florke bolster iiij blancketts ij payer of shoote & ij cuvleds — xxxs
Item ij platters ij pottingers j salt & ij sawsers — iijs vjd
Item j tong j malt seve & j bowd keever — xijd
Item j payer of hangells & j fring pann — viijd
Item iij coffers — vs
Item j grater & j brusse — iiijd
Item his wearing parrell — xxs
John wooley by Dett — xxxiijs
Thomas ffisher the yonger by Dett — Cs
Willm Donkin by band — xxs
John Nicholls — xxs
Item in money — iijs

Some is xviij li xviijs iijd

Probate Inventories

(The reference numbers are those of the
Wiltshire and Swindon Archives WSA)

GENTRY

Christopher Bayly   (Trowle) Gent   1687   P2/B/1093

9 cows, one steer, 2 heifers	£36
Three hay ricks	£14
Two mares and a gelding colt	£8
16 sheep, 2 hogs, 5 breeding pigs	£7 10s

Barn
A cart, a dung pot, plough harness with lumber goods   £7 6s 8d

Old House
A dough trough and other goods   10s

Kitchen
Pewter, brass and iron and other goods   £11 7s 2d

Buttery
10 barrels, one table, 2 dozen bottles and other goods   £3 3s 6d

White House
A cheese press, 2 cowls, a churn and other goods   £1 10s 6d

His wearing apparel   £10
Two feather beds, 3 flock beds with bedsteads and furniture belonging   £25

Kitchen Chamber
A spruce chest, a table and chest of drawers and other goods   £3 10s 6d

Cheese Loft
Cheese, wool, cheese boards and weights and scales and other goods.
        £7 10s 7d

Old Chamber
2 trunks, one chest and other goods   £1 6s 8d

Closet
A silver tankard, a gilt bowl with some pieces of plate and other goods

     £13 6s 8d

Table linen with sheets and other linen   £6 3s 4d

Brewhouse
One furnace with brewing vessels   £2 10s

At Turleigh: 30 bushels of wheat, 2 rick staddles, helm and straw besides
   other goods   £7 13s

The estate at Trowle   £400

Total £566 8s 9d

YEOMEN

John Bailey   **(Cumberwell)**   **Yeoman 1598**   **P2/B/193**

Hall
2 table boards, 2 stools, one cupboard   10s

One musket and one culver furnished   £1 10s

Parlour
One table board, one sideboard, 6 joined stools   £1 6s 8d

3 carpets and 6 cushions   £1

Great Chamber
One bedstead, 3 curtains and 1 tester, one chair, one table board, 2 coffers

     15s

One arras coverlet and 3 pillows   £2 10s

3 coverlets and one pair of blankets   £1

2 feather beds and one flock bed   £4

Little Chamber

2 bedsteads, one joined form	10s
One feather bed and one flock bed	£3
8 coverlets and 2 pairs of blankets	£3

Black Chamber

2 bedsteads, one flock bed and one press	£1 10s
2 coverlets and one pair of blankets	3s 4d

Cheese Loft

3 cheese racks and one pair of scales	16s
One hundred and three score cheeses and 40lbs of butter	£4 14s
3 weights of wool and one chest	£2 2s

Kitchen

One furnace and 8 brass pans	£4
3 brass kettles and 6 brass pots	£2 6s
3 skillets, 2 chaffing dishes and one spice mortar	11s
3 spits, 2 pair of andirons, 4 hangells, 3 skimmers, 2 frying pans, 2 dripping pans	16s
One fire fork, one fire pan, 2 brandirons	3s 4d

Buttery

One cupboard, 9 barrels and 15 candlesticks	30s
7 dozen pewter and 6 silver spoons	£4 10s
One basin and ewer and 4 flour pots	2s 6d
6 table cloths, 12 napkins, 6 towels	£1 12s
9 pairs of sheets, 4 pairs of pillow cases	£3 8s
5 salt tubs, 6 cheese vats and one malt mill	17s
Brewing vessels of all sorts	£1

His wearing apparel   £1

One wain, one iron bar, 3 pick forks, one spade, one pick axe	£2 6s
2 fat oxen and 12 kine	£35
6 young beasts and one mare	£12
50 sheep and lambs	£8

16

10 pigs and 12 poultry   £5
One stack of wheat, 17 load of barley, 7 load of oats, 2 stacks of hay   £45
Lease of the parsonage of Cumberwell   £6

Total   £135 8s 10d

William Joseph	Yeoman	1618	P2/IJ/71

Parlour

One table board and 6 joined stools   12s
One flock bed, one feather bed, one feather bolster, 2 feather pillows, 2 flock
   bolsters, 8 table napkins, 5 pair of sheets, 3 board cloths, 4 pillow cases,
   one bolster case, 2 pair of blankets, 3 coverlets, one flasket   £7 15s 8d

Hall

One table board with a joined form, 2 forms, one chair, 2 joined stools,
   7 pewter plates, 2 pewter candlesticks, 9 saucers, 3 pewter dishes,
   3 pottingers, one cup, one salt cellar, 2 dozen spoons, one pair of
   and irons, one pair of dogs, one pair of bellows   £1   14s

Kitchen

2 crocks, 4 brass kettles, 4 skillets, one brass ladle, 2 broaches, 2 pair of
   pothooks, one fire pan, one tongs, one frying pan, one gridiron, one brass
   candlestick, one cleaver, one skimmer, 2 pairs of hangells, one brand iron,
   2 tubs, one spinning turn, one lead bowl, 4 flitches of bacon   £4 6s 8d

Hall Chamber

One chest, 3 coffers, one flock bed, one flock bolster, one coverlet, one pair of
   blankets, one bedstead, 8 glasses   £1 10s 10d

Parlour Chamber

2 livery bedsteads, 2 [------], 1 shovel, 8 bushels of malt, 4 cheeses, 2 boards,
   one reel, 2 bills, one hook. 2 hatchets, one cutting knife, one draw knife,
   2 borers, one hammer,one pair of pincers, one chisel, one hand
   saw, 2 kipes, 4 wooden hooks, 4 hand staves   £2 1s

Dairy House

5 tubs, one kiver, one kive	11s
4 barrels	5s
One lantern, one sheeps crook, 2 picks	1s 2d
One range, 3 timber bowls, one peck, one search	6s
2 raying sieves, 2 malt sieves	1s 6d
2 saddles , one pannel	6s 8d
Timber platters and dishes	2s
4 earthen pans, 4 crocks	1s
2 dozen trenchers, one chopping board, one coping knife	1s 4d
3 kine	£9
2 pigs	£1
4 hens and one cock	2s 6d
His wearing apparel	£4 10s
3 acres of corn	£2 10s
Due to me by bonds from several men	£84

Total   £127 4s

Thomas Black (Trowle)	**Yeoman**	**1643**	**P2/B/683**

Hall

One table board with a frame, 2 joined forms, one side cupboard with other
implements   £3
2 Bibles and other books   £1

Parlour

One table board with a frame, 8 joined stools, one standing bedstead with
one feather bed and his furniture and other implements   £6

Kitchen

One cupboard and one safe with other implements   £1
One furnace   £1 6s 8d
One brass pan, 4 kettles, 4 brass pots, 4 skillets and other implements   £4 7s

Mill House

One malt quern, one great wooden silt with other implements   £1 6s 8d

18

Buttery

One beer horse, 6 barrels with other implements	£1
Pewter of all sorts	£1 10s

Loft over the Kitchen

Board bedstead, bed with his furniture and other implements	£1 10s

White House

One side board, milk pans and other implements	16s

Chamber over the Parlour

All his wearing apparel, both linen and woollen	£7
One standing bedstead, one feather bed with his furniture	£5
One chest	9s
One press to hold clothes, 2 coffers with other implements	16s

Chamber over the Hall

One livery bedstead, one low bedstead, one feather bed, one flock bed with bolsters belonging with other implements	£6 3s
6 pairs of sheets of all sorts	£3
3 board cloths, 14 table napkins, 6 pair of pillow cases	£1 6s

Cheese Loft

Malt and a quern	£4 10s
Cheese, bacon and wool and other implements	£7 6s

Corn on the ground of all sorts	£26
Hay	£16 10s
Wood and boards	£5 10s
6 horse beasts and one sucking colt	£13 10s
Wains, dung pots and other horse and plough harness	£7 13s 6d
14 milk kine	£36
9 young beasts and 5 weanling calves	£16 16s 8d
Sheep and lambs 90	£17 10s
10 pigs and troughs	£4 1s 8d
Geese and poultry	6s 8d
Ready money	£13 15s

Due upon bond from George Smith	£10
Due from: William Hunte	£4
William Coales	£2
Joseph White	8s
John Stallard the first day of August past	£1 7s

A chattel estate in the tenement where Thomas Black, above named,
did live in Trowle   £500

Desperate debts

Richard Pryer	5s
Anthony Chepman	11s
Thomas Barton for one bushel and a half barley	4s

Total   £793 0s 8d

Anthony Rogers (Woolley)   Yeoman   1667   P2/R/294

His wearing apparel   £1 10s

Kitchen

Pewter and brass and other lumber   £3

Chamber over the Kitchen

One bed with the furniture thereto belonging, 2 chests, 2 coffers and one box
£3

Chamber over the White House

One bed, cheese and other lumber   £3

White House

Cheese and other lumber   £4 6s 8d

Chamber over the Hall

A kettle with barrels and other lumber	£1 10s
2 flitches of bacon	£2

A parcel of threshed peas in the barn	£2
17 cows	£515
barren beasts	£10

7 yearlings	£6
8 calves and 3 pigs	£5
15 acres of wheat upon the ground, one acre of barley and 2 acres of pease	£24
The beans in the orchard	£1 10s
Wood in the backside	10s

Total   £119 6s

Robert Sartain (Great Trowle) Yeoman   1671   P1/C/301

(Hall)

2 kettles, 3 skillets, one skimmer, one flagon, one pint cup, half a dozen
pewter, 2 salts, one pewter candlestick, one little pewter dish, 6 chairs, one
table board with 2 trestles, one salt box, one cradle, 2 pair of andirons, one
fire pan, one pair of tongs, 2 pairs of hangells, one frying pan and 6 flitches
of bacon   £5 10s

Parlour

One table board with frame and one form   6s 8d

Whitehouse

4 tubs, 5 trendles, 4 barrels, one churn, one cheese press, 3 pails   £1 5s

His wearing apparel   £2 10s

Parlour Chamber

One feather bed, one pair of sheets, one bolster, 2 pillows and cases, one
coverlet, one chest, 2 coffers   £1 10s

Hall Chamber

2 flock beds, 2 bolsters, 2 bedsteads with cord and mat, 2 pairs of blankets,
one rug, one coverlet   £1 10s

Cheese loft

8 hundred of cheese   £8

The wheat and helm in the barn	£1
13 cows	£30
13 young beasts	£13
5 horses and one colt and their tackling	£10
4 pigs	£1 10s
One wagon, one sullow and all the harness belonging	£3
One gun	3s
14 tons of hay	£12
3 acres of wheat in the field with some small lumber about the house	£2

Total   £94   4s   8d

John Lydiard	**Yeoman**	**1675**	**P2/L/336**

His wearing apparel	£6
Owed him on a bond	£100
One small chattel determinable on one life	£15
All his corn and hay	£12 2s
6 cows, 2 heifers, 3 weanling calves	£22 10s

Parlour

One bed and one bedstead with all bed clothes and bedding together with all other household goods £10 19s

Chamber over the parlour and the little Closet

One standing bedstead, one truckle bedstead with all the bedding and all other goods £9 9s

Chamber over the hall

One bedstead, 2 beds with the bedding, one trunk, 2 chests, 2 coffers	£6
One silver tankard with some other plate	£6 13s

Hall

2 table boards and frames, with the joined stools, chairs and forms and implements of brass and iron with all other goods £3 3s

22

Buttery

All brass and pewter and all other utensils of wood, brass and iron   £6 7s 6d

All his linen   £2 6s

Brewhouse

One furnace and other lumber   £1 10s

Outhouse and out of doors

One pump together with a parcel of wood and all other lumber   £4 12s

Cheese Loft

One parcel of cheese with some other implements   £1 18s 6d

2 hogs and pigs   £3
The right in his coppice held from his death to Michaelmas   £4

Total   £215 10s

William Coles (Great Trowle)   Yeoman   1686   P2/C/774

Hall

One table board and frame, one cupboard, one settle, 2 joined stools, one
  form, one little table board, one other form, 3 chairs, one salt tub, one
  bacon rack, 2 spits, 2 pair of tongs, 2 hangells, 2 pair of andirons, 13
  pewter plasters, 9 pewter dishes, 2 flagons, 2 salts, 2 pewter candlesticks,
  one frying pan, one fire pan, 2 other candlesticks   £3 10s 6d

Chamber over the Entry

One tester bedstead, one bed with bedding, one chest, one sack of wheat   £4

Chamber over the White House

One tester bedstead with bedding, one cupboard, one table board and frame,
2 chairs, one joined form, 2 chests, 2 coffers, 3 boxes, one cushion with other
  lumber   £5
2 pairs of chains, one line, one pillion   6s

Chamber over the Buttery

One tester bedstead with a bed and bedding, one truckle bedstead with
bedding, one bolster, one press, 6 hundred of cheese, 3 fleeces of wool,
one parcel of locks   £9

Cheese Loft

One cheese rack, 13 hundred of cheese, 8 elm boards with other lumber
£7 5s

Room next the Hall

3 brass pans, one warming pan, 5 brass pots, 3 skillets, one brass chaffing
dish, one pestle and mortar, 2 forms, one saddle   £3 12s

Buttery

4 barrels, 2 wooden horses with other lumber   10s

Entry

One furnace, one form   £1

White House

13 tacks, 3 cheese vats , one brass pan, one brewing tub   £1 4s

Kitchen

2 cheese tubs, 4 trendles, one churn, one washing tub, one old coffer, 5 pails,
one cheese press, one fender, one dozen and a half trenchers   £1 8s 8d

Linen in the house
One holland sheet, 4 dowlas sheets, a pair of valences, 4 pillow cases,
6 table napkins, 2 table cloths, one wrought towel, one other table cloth,
one cupboard cloth, 6 silver spoons   £4 2s 6d

His wearing apparel   £5

Stall

One dung pot with other lumber   £1 10s

24

Barn

One parcel of wheat, one reed rake, one reap hook, one rack	12s

Backside

One old cart	£1
17 milch kine	£48
5 heifers two years aged	£8 15s
4 weanlings	£4
5 heifers three years aged	£12
2 fat hogs	£4
2 other pigs	£1 10s
4 horse beasts	£9
8 sheep	£2 8s
Money upon bond	£40
Other debts	£8 10s
Desperate debts	£8
Money due on rent	£1
Hay	£20
Corn upon the ground	£2 10s

Total   £215 3s 8d

Edmund Perry (Great Trowle)   Yeoman   1686   **P1/P/351**

Kitchen Chamber

His wearing apparel both woollen and linen	£5
2 beds and 2 bedsteads with their furniture	£6
2 rugs	£1 10s
3 chests and 3 coffers	£2 3s 4d

Hall Chamber

6 pairs of sheets	£1 19s
2 tablecloths and a dozen of napkins, 2 cupboard cloths, 5 pillow cases and all other small linen	£1 10s 9d
One coffer and one box	3s 4d
In some cheese	£2 2s

Buttery Chamber

6 bushels of wheat	17s 6d

Buttery

7 barrels	15s 2d
6 trendles, one churn	14s 6d
4 tubs, 7 pails, 2 rings with dishes and other small wooden vessels	£1 1s 5d
Milk pans and other earthen vessels	4s 10d

Hall

One table board and frame, one form and side cupboards	£1 0s 6d
One settle, 4 joined stools, 8 chairs	13s 4d
2 flitches of bacon and a piece and one chine	£1 5s 6d

Kitchen

One cupboard, one table board and frame, and one sideboard, a dozen cheese vats and one form and a bacon rack	9s 6d
7 brass crocks, one posnet, 3 skillets	£1 14s 6d
5 kettles, 2 brass pans, one warming pan, 3 brass candlesticks, one spice mortar and a basting ladle	£1 18s 6d
15 pewter platters, 2 pewter porringers, one flagon, one quart pot, 2 tankards, one salt	£2 2s 6d
One pair of andirons, 2 spits, 2 pairs of fire tongs, 2 fire pans, one beef pick, 3 pairs of pothooks, one gridiron, one steeling iron, 2 latten plates	6s 8d
2 hangells, one skimmer	2s
2 sacks and one grist bag	2s 4d
3 picks, one spade, one hatchet, one hook	3s 2d

In the pasture

17 kine	£51
4 heifers	£4 10s
4 yearlings	£2 10s
2 calves	15s
One mare with saddle and bridle	£3 10s
41 shearing sheep and two lambs	£1 19s
One sow and 7 pigs	£2 10s 4d
3 acres of wheat on the ground	£2 10s

One acre of pease on the ground	16s
7 bushels of barley	17s 6d
A stack of hay	£1 10s
Money in the house when he died	£40
One bond	£30
One bond	£5
One bond	£3 1s 9d
For lumber goods or anything forgotten	10s

Total   £189 19s 11d

Robert Harvey senior Yeoman   1688   P2/H/898

44 sheep	£13
2 cows and heifers	£7
4 oxen	£16
Waggon plough tackle	£12
8 horses and materials belonging to them	£25
Hay in the backside and a field for oats and beans	£7
2 hogs	£3
Peas	£4 10s
Wheat	£44
Vetches	£1
Barley	£12
12 acres of wheat in the fields growing	£12
Debts due	£50 4s 10
His wearing apparel and money in his purse	£10
3 chattel leases	£200
2 flitches of bacon	£1
The goods in the Hall and Buttery	£3
The goods in the Kitchen being brass and pewter	£3
3 bedsteads and bedding, 3 chests and a chair, a table board and other things in the Hall Chamber	£12

Total   £461 4s 10d

Henry Ballard (Frankleigh)   Yeoman   1690   **P2/B/1115**

---

16 acres of wheat @ £1 6s 8d per acre	£21 6s 8d
6 oxen	£23
14 cows	£42
2 young beasts	£2 10s
2 plough mares	£4 10s
2 colts	£5
One waggon, 3 ropes, 3 yokes, 6 bows	£7
One dung pot and wheels, one cutshide	£2 10s
One drag	8s
One pair of harrows	8s
5 hog pigs	£2 10s
2 felloes with coulters and shares	13s 4d
One rick staddle	6s
2 pairs of whipples, 2 pairs of hamses , one snaffle bridle, one saddle, 2 lines	
	16s

Hall Chamber

2 feather bolsters, 2 feather pillows, one flock bolster, 2 rugs, one set of
  curtains and valences, one bolster case, one sheet, one round table, one
  box, one rush chair   £2 2s 6d

Parlour Chamber

One half head bedstead, 2 flock beds, one mat, one cord, one flock bolster,
  one feather bolster, one rug, one coffer, one box   £1 17s

Broad Chamber

33 cheeses   £1

Servants Chamber

One flock bed and bolster, one bolster case, 3 blankets, one high bedstead,
  one truckle bedstead with cords and mats   15s

Buttery

2 half hogsheads, one tub, one wooden tray, 2 forms and one wooden horse
  whereon barrels stand   13s

Out Buttery

3 brass kettles, 2 brass pots, one brass skillet, one skimmer weighing 47 pounds at 10d a pound £1 19s 2d

One bell metal pot weighing 19 pounds at 7d a pound 11s 1d

One frying pan, one shove, one pair of pothooks, 2 forms and one dozen and a half of trenchers 3s

Larder

2 trendles, one tub, 3 pails, one butter basket, one pair of scales and one ring 12s

Dairy House

One cheese press and 9 cheese vats 10s

Parlour

One cheese tub, one brewing tub, one trendle, one table board, one old pipe, 4 barrels, one wooden bottle, one barrel horse 17s

Hall

One table board and a frame, 2 rush chairs, one pair of dogs, one fire pan, one pair of tongs, one spit, one gridiron 7s

4 pewter dishes, 4 pewter porringers, one tankard, one basin, one flagon, one salt, one pewter bottle, one pewter candlestick weighing 23 pounds at 7d a pound 13s 5d

Due from Walter Grant £3

His wearing apparel £1

Total £128 18s 2d

John Geatly   **Yeoman**   **1696**   **P2/G/566**

His wearing apparel   £3

Kitchen

One pewter tankard, 2 pewter platters, 6 pewter plates, one basting ladle 10s
One pair of tongs, one fire pan, one pair of iron dogs and one frying pan 6s
6 chairs   5s
One gun or fowling piece   10s
One salt box   6d
One pair of bellows, 2 wooden bowls, 6 spoons   1s 6d
One kettle, one warming pan, one skillet   12s

White House

3 cowls   2s 6d
4 pails   5s
3 trendles   6s
12 vats   6s
One cheese press   1s
One wooden horse and one barrel   3s 6d

Kitchen Chamber

One coffer   2s 6d
2 bedsteads, one bed case, one rug, one bolster   £1 5s
One trunk   5s

Cheese Loft

6 cheese shelves   5s
Leaden weights 8 and 20 pounds   3s 6d
300 cheeses at 1s 4d each   £20
2 pig troughs   1s
3 pigs   £3 15s

Hovel

One wash tub   1s

Stable

One black mare, 2 bridles, one saddle and pad	£5 5s

23 milch cows, 2 heifers, one bull, 4 yearlings, 4 ricks of hay and 2 stacks of hay all which were distrained by William Brewer for £86 16s for rent due and in arrears to him from the dead John Geatly at his death and were appraised by two appraisers at and sold for £118 out of which £86 16s due to Brewer being deducted, there remains £31 4s

Ready money	7s
Debts seperate and desperate	£4 16s 3¾d

Total   £73 10s 3¾d

Walter Perry   (Great Trowle) Yeoman   1698 — P2/P/669

His wearing apparel	£3

Hall

2 table boards, 12 joined stools, one cupboard, one chair	£1 16s
18 pewter platters	£1 5s 6d
One flagon, one tankard, one pewter candlestick	2s 2d
One pair of andirons	1s

Kitchen

6 kettles, 3 crocks, one frying pan	£3 12s 6d
2 skillets, one candlestick, one chaffing dish, one mortar	5s
4 broaches, one dripping pan, one fire pan, two pairs of hangells and other small utensils	6s 6d
One table board and frame, two forms, 3 chairs	5s
5 flitches of bacon and a bacon rack	£4 15s

White house

5 trendles, 2 tubs, 5 pails, 2 cheese presses	£1
In cheese vats and other utensils	5s

Buttery

2 brewing tubs, 4 barrels, one washing tub and other small utensils	12s

Cross Chamber
One bed and bedstead with the furniture	£2 10s 6d
One table board and frame, 3 coffers, one chest	£1 2s

Little Chamber
One bed and bedstead and the furniture	£3
One coffer, one chair	2s 2d

Hall Chamber
2 beds and bedsteads and the furniture, one coffer	£2 2s

Cheese Loft
2 silts, one powdering tub, 2 cheese racks, one tub	10s
Cheese, old and new	£1
Old iron	£2

Barn
Some old lumber	£1

Stall
Old lumber	£1 0s 6d

Stable
One rack, one manger, one wash tub, and other lumber	£1 15s

Wain House
One wagon, one cart and other tackling	£4

Yard
Wood, one piece of timber	£1

15 cows, 5 heifers, 4 yearlings, 3 calves	£59
2 mares, one colt	£6
2 pigs	£1 15s
One hay rick, one stack	£8
One chattel lease tenement	£25
The executors' half year in a copyhold tenement	£10

One acre of pease	15s
Ready money	£50
One bond and interest being a desperate debt	£7 14s
In small debts	£8
Lumber goods and things forgotten and unseen	5s
Due from Mary Coales	£1

Total   £215 16s 10d

HUSBANDMEN

Richard Colborne	**Husbandman**	**1552**	**P2/C/5**

Chamber

A feather bed, a flock bed, 2 coverlets	£1
3 pairs of sheets, a gown and a coat	13s 4d

Hall

2 crocks, 2 cauldrons, 2 pans, 8 pieces of pewter, a vessel, 2 candlesticks	16s
A table with appurtenances, a turn, a chair, a cupboard	6s 4d

In outward stuff

An old wain with appurtenances	16s

Beasts and cattle

4 oxen, 2 bullocks, one cow, 2 heifers	£6 13s 4d
28 sheep	£2
A mare and a colt	13s 4d
3 pigs	10s
In grain by estimation	£4

Total   £17 8s 4d

| **William Mathew** | **Husbandman** | **1580** | **P2/M/62** |

6 platters, 2 saucers	10s
One pan, one crock, one posnet, one cauldron and 3 skillets	£1
One broach, one rundire, one frying pan, one fire pick, 2 brand irons, one gridiron, one fleshhook	6s 8d
5 coffers, one cupboard, one table board and 2 chairs	£1
All treen vessels	£1
One feather bed with appurtenances to the same and 2 bedsteads	£2 13s 4d
The goodwife's apparel	£2
One saw and 2 borers	4s 4d
One yoke and 2 plough chains, one nipper, one hatchet, one sullow	10s
One bucket and a chain, 2 turns, one pair of cards	2s
Standing timber	£1 1s
Part of one wain	£1
One ox	£1 14s 4d
2 kine	£4 6s 8d
2 pigs	13s 4d
The part of one mare	5s
One heifer of a year old	13s 4d
3½ acres of wheat	£2 6s 8d
Barley and oats	10s
For meadow grass	£1

Total £22 14s 8d

| **Henry Bapshin** | **Husbandman** | **1585** | **P2/B/93** |

Hall

2 boards, 2 forms, 4 trestles, 2 stools	2s 6d
A bedstead, a flock bed, one pair of blankets, a coverlet, a bolster	13s 4d

Chamber within the Hall Chamber

A cupboard, a square board with a frame, a coffer	6s 8d
A latten basin, 8 platters, 3 pottingers, a pewter basin, 2 saucers, 2 salt cellars, 4 brass candlesticks, 6 spoons	10s

3 silver spoons	6s
2 coats, one doublet, 2 pair of hose, a cloak and 2 hats	£1

Chamber over the Hall

2 bedsteads, 2 flock beds, 3 blankets, 2 coverlets, 2 bolsters, one pillow, one coffer	£1

The further Chamber over the Hall

A bedstead, a shred coverlet, part of a blanket	2s
A parcel of fell wool	14s

Kitchen

3 brass pans	£1
3 crocks, one posnet, a frying pan	8s
3 broaches, 2 pair of crock hooks, 2 dripping pans, a cleaver, a gridiron, a chopping knife, a skimmer	7s
A pair of andirons, 2 brandirons, 2 crock hangells	4s

Kitchen Chamber

3 old witches, a kneading trough, a cheese rack	3s
5 barrels, one kiver, one cowl, one trendle	5s
A tenon saw, 4 wedges, one axe, 2 chisels, 2 borers, 3 hatchets, a hedge bill, 2 picks, 2 dung forks	6s
A brown bill, a bushel, a peck with other trash	3s 4d

Barn

2 loads of wheat and rye	£1
7 loads of dredge corn	£3
3 ladders	1s 8d

About the house and abroad in the leases

3 oxen	£7
22 ewe sheep and hogs	£2
2 yearling bullocks	£1 3s 4d
A young mare	£1 13s 4d
A gander and 6 geese	5s
3 hogs	15s

The poultry about the house	4s
A drake and 7 ducks	2s 8d
An iron bound wain, 3 yokes, 4 ropes	£3
A drag, 2 pair of aies	6s 8d
A dung pot, a load shield, posts and coverings for 2 ricks	6s 8d
10 loads of hay	£2
A yetting stone	3s 6d
A pack saddle and a girth	1s 6d

Field

9 acres and 3 yards of wheat, 2 acres and one yard of rye	£3

Total £33 14s 2d

John Fox (Trowle)   [Husbandman]   1590   P2/F/126

Hall

One table board, 2 trestles, one form	2s 6d
One cupboard with a chair	6s 8d
One painted cloth	8d

Lower Chamber

One bed with a pair of sheets, a bolster and a coverlet	£1

Chamber above

One feather bed with 2 coverlets, a pair of sheets and a bolster with a bedstead	£1
2 coffers, one press	7s
His wearing apparel	5s

Buttery

6 tubs	3s 4d
2 brass pans	16s
One furnace pan and a malting stone	13s 4d
2 kivers	1s 8d
6 platters	6s 8d
5 pottingers	2s 6d

5 saucers	1s
3 candlesticks with a posnet	3s 4d
4 cauldrons with a little pan	13s 4d
3 pails with a malt sieve	1s 3d
2 broaches, a gridiron, 3 andirons	5s
2 turns	1s

Folk Chamber

One bed with that as belongs to it	5s
One hangell, 2 pair of pothooks	1s
6 hens and one cock	2s 4d
2 geese and a gander	2s
The wheat in the barn	10s
Of wheat on the ground one acre and a half	13s 4d
4 yearlings	£2 13s 4d
One heifer of 2 years old	£1 5s
5 kine and a heifer	£13 6s 8d
3 flitches of bacon	10s
One sow and 2 little pigs	9s

Total   £25 2s 3d

Thomas Clarke   **1591**   **P2/C/90**

Hall

One table board with a frame, one bench with a wainscot backboard, one joined form, one other form	8s
2 cupboards, one chair, 2 joined stools	16s
One chest, one round table board, one little joined stool	6s 8d
4 latten basins, 2 pewter basins, one ewer, 2 quart pint pots, 4 flour pots, one little ewer, one half pint pot	4s
5 brass candlesticks, one pewter candlestick, one brass mortar and pestle, one brass chaffing dish	15s
Half a dozen cushions and a carpet cloth	£1 6s
The painted cloths and 2 cupboard cloths	5s

Chamber over the Hall

One table board, 2 trestles, 2 joined forms, 2 other forms, 2 cheese racks,
one rack for a basin to stand on   5s

One press, one chest plated with iron, one chair, one coffer, one form,
2 old coffers   16s

One standing bedstead, 2 other bedsteads, one truckle bedstead   10s

2 feather beds and 2 flock beds   £2 13s 4d

4 feather bolsters and 3 pillows   13s 4d

5 coverlets and 3 blankets   £1 10s

One pair of holland sheets, 3 pair of lockram sheets, 2 pillow cases,
2 table cloths, and half a dozen napkins   £2

One weight of wool   £1

Chamber within the Hall

One round table board, one chest and one press   5s

One bedstead with a tester and a stained cloth   3s

His wearing apparel   £1 10s

Buttery

One horse to set drink on, 5 barrels, 3 standards, 2 iron dibs, 2 measuring
vats, 3 pails, one powdering tub   6s 8d

One mustard mill   1s

Half a dozen pewter dishes, 3 dozen pewter spoons, one silver spoon   8s 4d

Half a dozen wooden dishes, 4 dozen trenchers   1s 4d

Half a dozen stone cups   1s

2 horse locks, one horse comb, one pair of shears, 3 rip hooks   2s 6d

Kitchen

5 brass pots, one posnet, one skillet   £1 5s

4 brass pans, 5 kettles, one brass ladle   £2 13s 4d

2 brass skimmers, one cleaver, one chopping knife, 2 gridirons, one flesh
hook   3s

3 broaches, one pair of andirons, 4 brand irons, one fire pan, one fire pick,
one dripping pan, one frying pan   £1

One pair of hangells, one pair of pot hooks, one pair of bellows   2s

One brewing horse, one cupboard, 2 turns, one pair of cards, one malt sieve,
one riddle, one ring, one flasket, one tankard   10s

One hatchet, one wood hook, one black bill, 3 iron wedges, one mattock,
2 little stones   5s

The beam scales and weights — 2s 6d
One cheese ring, 3 cheese vats — 2s
One rick staddle — 5s
22 boards — 15s

Cattle

3 kine — £7
2 horses — £3
One mare and a colt — £2 6s 8d
16 sheep and 5 lambs — £3 13s 4d
2 pigs — 8s
One hen — 4d

Corn and grass

5 acres of wheat — £3 6s 8d
7 acres of barley — £3 5s
By estimation, 4 acres of grass — £1 13s 4d

Debts owing

Thomas Thackam, vicar — £1 1s
Roger Golledge — 15s
Richard Reynold alias Westbury — 10s
Richard Steere — 4s
Robert Fyppe — 6s 8d
Thomas Silbee — 3s 4d
Widow Mason — 2s 6d
Robert Keere — 2s 6d
Richard Brown, butcher — 4s 6d
Widow Ryder — 4s
James Hillgrove — 2s
James Battill — 2s 6d
John Jones, carrier — 6s 8d
James Rogers — 10s
William Harford — 13s 4d
John Mathew, tucker — £1
Robert Rundill owes at Michaelmas come two years — £20

Total £78 5s 4d

Thomas Stevens (Trowle)   Husbandman   1593   P2/S/149

Hall
One table board, one form, one stained cloth   2s 8d
One cupboard, one chair   4s 10d

House within the Hall
One table board, one form, 2 trestles, one old coffer   2s 8d

Chamber over the Kitchen
One flock bed, one pair of canvas sheets, one coverlet, one bolster with a
   bedstead   13s 4d
One floor of malt   10s

Chamber over the Hall
One feather bed, 2 bolsters, 2 pillows, one coverlet, one pair of sheets with a
   bedstead   £1 6s 8d
2 coffers, 2 bushels of oats, 2 sacks   5s 8d
3 pairs of canvas sheets   10s
One canvas board cloth and 2 pillows   3s 4d
His wearing apparel   £1

Next Chamber within
8 bushels of malt   13s 4d

Kitchen
One old bedcase, one coverlet, one pair of canvas sheets with a bedstead
                                                                6s 8d
One pan and 6 small kettles   £1 4s
4 small pots and one skillet   £1
One andiron and one broach   1s 8d
3 standards, 2 cowls, 3 pails, one churn, one half bushel   6s 8d
3 trendles, 2 tubs, one quern for malt   11s 8d
One malt sieve and 3 ring sieves   1s
6 platters   5s
8 pottingers, 6 saucers, 2 salt cellars   6s 8d
3 brass candlesticks   3s

16 acres of wheat sown at an out rent	£5 6s 8d
6 acres more of wheat on his own land	£3 10s

Bakehouse

Ruff	£2
30 bushels of barley	£2 5s
One brandiron, one gridiron, one pair of hangells, 2 pair of pothooks	2s 4d
2 geese and a gander, one cock and 6 hens	6s
2 turns, one tenon saw	1s 8d
One mow of wheat	£5
One mow of hay	£1 6s 8d
One wain and plough harness	£2
3 oxen	£8
5 kine	£10
4 young beasts and 3 yearlings	£5
One mare	£1
One sow and 8 shoots	£1 10s
4 sheep	13s 4d

Total   £58 1s 2d

William Raynoldes alias Westbery Husbandman 1598   P2/R/67

Hall

3 table boards, one form and one bench	10s
One cupboard, one chair, 3 stools, one form and one cradle	8s
One firepan, a pair of tongs, one pair of hangells, one iron crook, one gridiron, one toasting iron, one frying pan and a pair of bellows	4s 8d
The third part of a furnitude, one jack, one sword and 2 daggers	18s

Buttery

One horse, one bench, 2 tacks, one stool and 2 barrels	4s
2 dozen trenchers, half a dozen dishes and one tankard	8d
One brass mortar and pestle and 2 brass candlesticks	4s 6d
One charger, 6 platters, 5 pottingers, one salt, one tin cup and 3 saucers	10s 8d

Great Buttery

2 horses, one pair of trestles, 2 benches, one chopping board and one stool
8d
4 bottles and one riding saddle and one bridle 6s 8d
One kype, one malt sieve, one pair of whipples, one wain line and one tang
5s
2 kyves, 3 cowls, one barrel, one churn, one bowl, one powdering tub, one
peck and 4 pails 10s
6 boards, one yoke and old timber 6s
One ring, one lantern, one broach, one flesh hook, one skimmer, one
chopping knife and one toasting iron 2s

Cellar

One bench, one tack, one form and one cheese ring 6d
2 kyvers, 2 raying sieves, one search and one cheese vat 4s
One salt trough with a cover 4s
2 brass crocks, 2 cauldrons, one posnet, one skillet and one pair of pothooks
£1 6s 8d
3 stone troughs and 2 sacks of lime 10s
One stone trough, one packsaddle and one girth 1s

Kitchen

One malt mill, one hen coop, one oil pipe and 2 planks 8s

Corn Chamber

One joined table with a frame, 2 forms, one press and one plank 10s
One bedstead, one flock bed, one bolster, coverlet and one blanket 16s

Broad chamber

One bedstead, one coverlet, 2 blankets and one bolster 6s 8d
6 planks 10s
One witch, one vat and one spinning turn 6s 8d

Wool loft

One bedstead, one flock bed, 2 peels, one coverlet and 2 blankets £1

Porch Chamber

One joined bedstead, one flock bed, one bolster, one coverlet, one pair of blankets and one mat	£1 10s
One bedstead, one bolster, one coverlet and 2 blankets	6s 8d
His wearing apparel	£2
3 coffers, one form, one chair, one box and one black bill	6s
One pair of sheets, 2 board cloths, 2 pillows and 2 table napkins	£1 6s 8d

Malt loft

One cheese rack, one form, one tack and 2 kypes	2s
9 pounds of black wool and 3 pounds of flock	6s 9d
2 forks, 2 rakes and 2 picks	1s
One iron bar, one hoe, one hatchet, one spoke shave and other tools and old iron	10s

Barton

4 yokes, 4 ropes, 2 felloes, one pair of aies, one dray, one seed lip and one old wain bed	£1 4s
One iron bound wain, one dung pot and one load shield	£1
2 rick staddles and 2 ladders	8s
All the plough timber	£1
4 pig troughs	4s
2 cocks, 4 hens, 2 geese and 4 goslings	6s

The Cattle

One sow and 2 pigs	13s 4d
6 oxen	£20
6 kine	£13 6s 8d
2 mares and one colt	£5
24 sheep	£6 13s 4d
4 young beasts	£3
3 calves	£1
15 lambs and 2 hogs	£3

The Corn

All the crop of corn upon the ground	£55

Total	**£128 18s 9d**

John Hilman   (Trowle)   [Husbandman]   1603   P2/H/213

Hall

One table board and a form with a little square board	3s 4d
A cupboard	6s 8d
A chair stool	1s
The Bible and other books	2s

Chamber next the Hall

A standing bedstead and certain furniture to the same belonging	18s
2 coffers	2s

Chamber over the Hall

A standing bedstead and certain furniture to the same belonging	£1
A table board, a board bedstead, one coffer	2s 6d
A weigh beam and certain weights of lead, a cheese board and a cheese rack	4s 6d
6 green cheeses	1s 6d

Buttery or little house next the Hall

3 brass pots and a skillet	10s
2 cauldrons	10s
2 brass pans	13s 4d
4 platters, 2 porringers, 3 candlesticks and a small spice mortar	7s 6d
One board cloth	2s

House next the Hall

A small stone, a lie store and a cheese ring	13s 4d

Barn

By estimation 3 loads of all sorts of corn	£2 13s 4d
The hay	£2
2 loads of vetches	10s
A wain bound with iron and certain plough harness to the same belonging	£2

Cattle

2 oxen	£6

3 kine and a heifer	£8
4 young beasts	£4 13s 4d
A mare and her colt	£1 10s
2 weanling calves	£1
6 geese	3s
3 ducks, 3 hens, a cock	3s
In pigs about the house	£1
A brandiron, hangells and pothooks	1s 4d
His wearing apparel	13s 4d

Debts owing to him

William Howse of Trowbridge	13s
Henry Davis of Bradford	10s
Robert Cooper of Trowle	4s
Robert Whiting of Trowle	4s

Debts owing by him

To Thomas Prior of Trowle	£1

Total   £36 16s

John Hendy senior   (Trowle) Husbandman   1618   P2/H/325

Hall

A table board with a form and other implements	2s

Chamber within the hall

2 bedsteads, 2 beds, one coverlet, 2 pair of sheets and 2 bolsters	£1 10s

Chamber over the Hall

2 chests with other lumber	10s

Buttery

3 barrels with other implements	10s

Kitchen

Brass and pewter with other implements	£1 10s

Mill House

2 tubs, one silt stone with other implements	10s
His wearing apparel	£2
Plough harness	£4
Corn in the barn	£5 10s
Wheat	£4
Hay	£2 10s
Wheat upon the ground	£3
3 oxen	£14
2 kine, one calf	£4
2 young heifers	£3
One pig	13s 4d
2 mares	£4
Bees and poultry	6s 8d

Total   £51 12s

John Barton   (Widbrook)   Husbandman 1628   P2/B/502

Hall and Inner Chamber

One table board, a form, one old cupboard, a chair, cradle, stools and other lumber	10s
3 chests, one wainscot bedstead, one little table board	£1

Chamber over the Hall

3 bedsteads, one chest with other lumber	£1
4 hundred of cheese	£4
4 beds with bolsters, 2 pillows and 6 coverlets	£7
One weight of wool	£1
2 pairs of sheets, 4 pillows, dozen of napkins, 3 meat cloths, a bearing sheet with swatchband	£3
One dozen pewter vessels great and small, one quart pot, 2 candlesticks, 3 salt cellars, one spice mortar and pestle	£1
2 crocks, 4 kettles, one skillet and one brass pan	£2 13s 4d

One cheese press, barrel and other lumber	10s
One saw, 2 wedges, 2 hangells, pothook, frying pan with other lumber	10s

Without doors

Pease, barley, malt and other grain	£3 10s
3 bacon pigs, one flitch	£3 10s
4 breeding pigs	£2
Poultry	10s
One rick of corn and hay	£10
Wheat and barley in the barn	£5
The malt mill, wain, plough harness, ladders, wood with other outstuff	£8
6 oxen	£30
12 kine	£30
4 young beasts	£8
4 yearling calves	£2 10s
3 horsebeasts with hackney tackling	£7
100 sheep	£38
14 acres of wheat growing	£12
His wearing apparel	£6
Debts owing upon specialty	£50
Ready money in the house	£20

Total (not given)   [£157 13s 4d]

William Archard senior [Husbandman] 1631   P2/A/154

Inner Chamber

One standing bed and bedstead, one bolster, 3 pillows, 2 coverlets, one blanket	£2
One press, 3 coffers, one box, 2 tacks	10s

Upper Chamber

One tack, one bedstead and bed, one bolster, one coverlet — 10s

One cheese rack, one kneading trough, one coffer, one pair of scales with
   other household implements — 3s 4d

Hall

One table board, 2 forms, 2 chairs, one cupboard — 15s

8 platters, 3 porringers, 2 brass candlesticks, half a dozen saucers,
   2 pewter dishes, 2 drinking cups, one brass mortar, one salt — 16s

One bench, one pair of andirons, 2 hangells, one fire pan and tongs,
   one broach and gridiron — 5s

Cheese — 6s

Kitchen

2 brass pots, one skillet, 4 kettles, 2 brass pans, one pair of pothooks — £2

White House

3 barrels, one churn, 3 tubs, one powdering tub, 2 tacks with other household
   implements — 6s

Kitchen Chamber

One bedstead, one bed with a bolster, 2 coverlets, 2 blankets — £2

2 pairs of sheets, 3 pillow cases, half a dozen napkins, 2 board cloths,
   one chest — £2 2s

His wearing apparel — £1

One cheese ring — 2s

One breeding pig — 8s

One chattel lease — £21

4 rudder beasts — £8 10s

Wood — 3s

Hay — £2

Total   £44 16s 4d

48

Hall
One plain table board with trestles, one form, 2 chairs, 2 stools and one cradle
6s 8d
Bacon there
£1

White House
4 little barrels, one churn, 3 pails, kivers, earth vessels, dishes and trenchers
with other small implements
£1
2 kettles, 2 crocks, one skillet, one platter, 4 porringers with other small things
£2

Chamber over the White House
3 flock beds with their furniture
£4
One standing bedstead with3 other bedsteads, one chest, 2 coffers
£2
His wearing apparel
£4

12 oxen
£60
2 wains with iron bound wheels, 3 sullows and drags and aies with all other
things thereunto
£10
6 kine
£22
2 horses
£8
100 sheep and 32 lambs
£25
14 pigs little and great
£4
19 acres of corn of all sorts
£20
All the corn in the barn
£4

Debts owing upon accounts from several parties
£14
Monies in the house
£3 10s

Total   £183 16s 8d

| **Thomas Kelson** | **Husbandman** | **1681** | **P2/K/233** |

His wearing apparel and money £7

13 rudder beasts	£26
18 sheep	£5
3 mares, one colt	£8
3 hogs	£4
25 acres of corn	£33 10s
8 loads of hay	£12
A rick of mangfodder	£1 10s
Plough harness	£7
2 whole rick staddles with some spare stones	£1 15s
4 dozen of holm	10s
2 yetting stones, a bucket and chain for the well	£1 6s 8d
A malt mill	£2
A rick staddle in the barn	16s
A stack of boards with some planks	£1
3 tallets	£3
Some old wheat in the barn	£3
3 ladders	4s
70 small cheeses	£1 15s

Hall

2 table boards, one form, 4 stools, one chair and other lumber £1 15s

Kitchen

A table board, a settle, a bacon rack and other small things £1 10s
A furnace and grate £2

Buttery

Barrels, horses, tubs, a cheese press, churn with other small things £3 10s
The inner door, glass and window leaves £1

Chamber over the Kitchen

One feather bed and bolster, a flock bed, a bedstead, a rug, a pair of blankets
£6 10s

A chest, a coffer, a box, a chair, a press, a table board £1 10s

Chamber over the Hall

3 bedsteads, 3 flock beds and bolsters, coverlets and blankets, 2 coffers

£4 15s

Chamber over the Buttery

2 flock beds and bolsters, one bedstead £1 13s 4d

One carpet, 4 cushions and some linen £1 10s

A weight of wool £1

3 spits, a pair of andirons, 3 pair of hangells, 3 pair of pothooks and other
 small things £1

A flitch of bacon 10s

33 lb of pewter at 10d the lb £1 7s 6d

72 lb of kettle brass at 10d the lb £3

60 lb of crock brass at 6d the lb £1 10s

2 chattel leases £67

The executors time on the 3 copyholds £1

A small debt due 8s

2 table boards in the new house 10s

Total £219 6s 6d

Edward Naish (Frankleigh Farm) [Husbandman] 1692   P1/N/104

Parlour

One table board and two chairs with other utensils 10s

Kitchen

One settle, one trencher rack and other utensils 8s

Buttery

3 barrels with other utensils 15s

Chamber over the Parlour

One bed with its furniture, one coffer with its utensils £1 4s

Chamber over the Kitchen

One bed with its furniture with other utensils	£2 6s
In brass and pewter	£6
In iron ware	5s
His wearing apparel	£5
In books	10s
In bacon and cheese	15s
6 ox beasts and 3 horse beasts, one wagon and one plough	£40
One pair of cart wheels	£3
27 acres of corn upon the ground	£27
40 couples of sheep	£17
Good debts and desperate debts	£570
Total	**£674 13s**

Daniel Kinton (Woolley)	**Husbandman 1696**	**P2/K/273**

His wearing apparel	£3
All his goods in the parlour	£1 5s
All his goods in the parlour chamber	£2 10s
Fourteen hundredweight of cheese at 17s a hundredweight	£11 18s
His linen	10s
His pewter	£1 5s
All his brass	£3 10s
All his wooden vessels	£1 4s
2 oxen, 12 cows, 2 young beasts, 45 sheep	£68
5 pigs	£5
All sorts of corn within doors	£11
All his hay	£15
All his wheat growing now on the ground	£7
The goods in the kitchen	10s
Total	**£131 12s**

CLOTH INDUSTRY

CLOTHIERS

John Smith   **Clothier   1667**   **P2/S/680**

Bed chamber

His wearing apparel   £6   13s   4d

3 chests, one side cupboard, one round table board, one box of drawers,
   one joined press, 3 cloth chairs, 4 joyned stools, one trunk, one pair of
   andirons, one pair of fire shovels and tongs, one pair of bellows   £6

One tester bedstead with curtains and valences, one truckle bedstead,
   one feather bed, 3 feather bolsters, 3 flock beds, 2 pair of blankets, 3 pair
   of pillows, one green rug and a red coverlet, 6 cushions, 3 carpet cloths,
   one flock bolster with divers small implements   £15

Chamber over the Hall

2 tester bedsteads, one half headed bedstead, one cupboard, 2 coffers, one
   box, one truckle bedstead, 2 flock beds, one green rug, one green coverlet,
   2 bolsters, 2 pillows, one pair of curtains and valences and 2 pair of blankets
                                                                    £7   10s

Little Chamber over the Buttery

One standing bedstead, one flock bed, one green rug, one pair of blankets,
   one bolster, one chair with other implements and one side cupboard   £3

Hall

One table board, 6 stools, one joined form, 6 leather chairs, 2 joined chairs,
   one side cupboard, one bigger cupboard, one round table, one pair of
   and irons, one pair of dogs, fire tongs, 6 cushions, one carpet cloth with
   other implements   £5

Buttery

2 hogsheads, 3 half hogsheads with other implements   £1   10s

Kitchen

3 table boards, one joined chair, one pair andirons, one jack, 3 spits, one iron
   dripping pan, one joined form with all other implements of wood and iron
                                                                         £2

4 brass pans, 3 brass crocks, one furnace, his pewter and all other vessels and
  implements of brass and pewter   £15

Lower House

All the brewing vessels and all the other vessels of wood with all lumber there
                                                              £1   13s   4d

30 of his white sorting clothes of his red and green mark at £5 10s per cloth
                                                                    £165
15 of his yellow copper mark cloths at £7 10s per cloth   £112 10s
8 packs of sorting warp and abb at £11 per pack   £88
14 bundles of fine abb at 5s per pound   £26   5s
5 score of coarse warp   £ 3   6s   8d
20 bundles of coarse abb   £20
6 score of list   £3
12 pounds of dyed list   12s
5 score of fine warp   £6 5s
Wool fleece and broke   £15

Wool loft

Weights, scales, warping bar and scirm and all other implements   £2
Oil   £3

One horse beast and 4 pigs   £7
A garner   £3
1 chattel lease in Bradford determined at the decease of John Smith,
  the son of the deceased   £150
His plate   £5
Linen   £5

                                    Total   £677   15s   4d

FULLERS

Anthony Mathew (Woolley)   Fuller   1605   P1/M/21

Hall

One table board with a frame, 2 joined stools, 2 trestles	5s
One cheese press, 3 pails, 3 trendles and 2 cowls	8s
5 barrels, one kive, 3 turns	8s 4d
One pair of hangells, one pair of andirons,one frying pan, one gridiron, 2 pair of pothooks, one dripping pan, one broach, one bellows	6s 8d
2 crocks	£1 10s
2 cauldrons, 2 brass pans, one skillet, one crock, one posnet	£1 10s 6d
2 beating hurdles, one reel, one cradle, 2 joined stools	4s 6d
2 old vats, 2 malt sieves, one ring, one search and 4 sieves	2s 6d
One table board, 2 benches	5s
One bag, one sack, one hatchet, one broach	1s 4d
One old cupboard and one powdering tub	4s 4d

Chamber over the Entry

One boarden bedstead with a flock bed, one bolster, one coverlet, 2 blankets	£1 6s 8d
3 baskets, one kype, 2 tacks, one weigh beam and scales, 6 leaden weights	8s
9 score pound of fine wool	£13 10s
Fine yarn	£2 10s
4 score pound of sorting wool	£3 10s
40 pound of list wool	£1
One lantern	8d

Chamber over the Hall

One joined table board with a frame, one joined form, one chair	10s
One chest, one cupboard, 2 boxes, 2 coffers	£1 5s 10d
One standing bedstead with a flock bed, one bolster, 2 coverlets, 2 blankets	£4
One truckle bedstead with a flock bed,one bolster, 2 blankets,one mat	£1 10s
3 pair of canvas sheets, one pair of holland sheets, 3 board clothes, half a dozen napkins, 3 towels, 4 pillows	£4 10s
5 platters, 6 pottingers, 2 candlesticks, 2 salts, 2 pewter dishes, one dozen spoons	16s 6d
Cheese and bacon	£1 13s 4d

The corn

The third part of 7 acres of wheat	£2 6s 8d
The third part of 6½ acres of barley and beans	£1 16s 8d
3 acres of barley and beans	£2 13s 4d
The corn in the barn	£1 6s 8d
Hay and helm	13s 4d
The poultry	2s 8d
One old wain bed and old iron	10s
The lease of 3 acres of ground	£1
One pack saddle, one serpler, a twig and girth	6s 4d
Due from Richard Pickering upon Michaelmas day next by bill	£2

The cattle

One mare and 2 colts	£7 13s 4d
4 kine	£9 10s
One bullock	13s 4d
7 sheep and 3 lambs	£2 6s 8d
3 pigs	£1
Wood and timber	£1 1s

Total £76 6s 4d

Robert Titt	**Fuller**	**1616**	**P1/T/42**

Chamber

An old table board and 2 forms	2s
A cupboard and a chest	4s
2 coffers, one barrel and a standard	6s
A bedstead and a flock bed	8s
2 coverlets, two blankets and a sheet	16s
2 old bolsters	2s
4 brass candlesticks, 2 pewter dishes and a little pewter cup	3s
7 pound of pewter and a salt	4s 4d
3 little crocks,2 cauldrons, 6 spoons	10s
A frying pan, a pair of hangells, a broach, a pothook	2s
All his wearing apparel	6s 8d

Shop

6 dozen of fullers handles	2s
A shearboard and 2 trestles, 2 pair of fullers shears	4s
A few clifts of wood	1s
A turn and a pair of cards	1s

Total   £3   12s

John Nash senior   Fuller   1627   P2/N/97

One flock bed		6s
One bolster		1s
One more bolster		2s
One pillow		1s
2 coverlets		5s
2 blankets		4s
A half head bedstead cord and mat		4s
One coaster	1s	6d
A short table board and form	3s	4d
One trendle	1s	8d
2 small crocks and a kettle		12s
One barrel and a cowl	2s	4d
3 old bowls, 2 treen platters and a dish		8d
2 pewter platters	1s	4d
One brandiron, a pair of tongs, a fire pan, a hangells, a broach		2s
An elm chair		6d
All his apparel		£1
Monies in house		£1
In Henry Aborns hand		£7

Total   £11   8s   4d

Robert Shadwell   **Fuller**   **1635**   **P1/S/237**

Hall

One table board, one form and one chair	5s
One crock and 3 kettles	10s
2 brass pans	11s
3 small iron dogs, a pot hangell, one frying pan, one pair of hangells	3s
One basin, 3 platters, 2 saucers, one pewter candlestick, one tin bottle and a small brass candlestick, one small goblet and one salt cellar	6s
One trendle, one tub, one pail, one pair of bellows, one spinning turn, one reel with other lumber	4s

Chamber

One half-headed bedstead, mat and cord, one chest and 3 coffers	15s
One flock bed, one bolster, one coverlet, 3 blankets	£1 10s
One board cloth, 3 sheets, one napkin	12s
In the backside, certain wood	3s
Certain debts owing	£38
Wearing apparel	13s 4d
One weigh beam and scales	1s
2 brass candlesticks and one chaffing dish	4s

Debts left to pay

To Anthony Fuller	£10
To John Grant	£10
Funeral expenses	£2

(No total given)

John Ivyleaf　　　　　**Fuller**　　　　　**1638**　　　　　**P2/IJ/85**

Shop

The wares with all the appurtenances thereto belonging　　　　　£10

Hall

One lardy tableboard with a little sideboard, one standing cupboard
　　with 2 chairs, 4 stools and the wainscot　　　　　£2

Chamber over the Hall

3 bedsteads　　　　　£1
One tableboard, one press, 2 chests and one little box and a form　£1 3s 4d
3 flock beds with 3 bolsters, 4 pillows, 6 coverlets and 6 blankets　£7

The linen

3 pairs of sheets, 3 pairs of pillow cases, 2 bolster cases, 3 tablecloths,
　　one dozen napkins　　　　　£3

One dozen pewter, 3 candlesticks, one bowl, one salt cellar, one beaker　£1 10s
3 crocks, 2 kettles, 2 brass pans, 3 skillets, one posnet and one skimmer
　　　　　£2 10s

The Loft over the Shop

A beam and scales and leaden weights with an old chest, one hacking saddle
　　with other lumber　　　　　£1

The iron work with the back　　　　　£1
The wood pile with coals, boards and other lumber　　　　　£3
One Bible with other books　　　　　6s 8d
His wearing apparel　　　　　£3

His leases of his house and other tenements　　　　　£20
Debts owing him　　　　　£20
Ready money　　　　　£10

Total　£86 10s

CLOTHWORKERS

Edward Coely	**Clothworker**	**1677**	**P1/C/331**

His wearing apparel	£1
One flock bed with all apparel and appurtenances thereto belonging	£2
One chest, a coffer, a settle, a box and other implements in the Chamber	
	£1 2s 6d
All his brass and pewter	£2

Hall

A table board, a cupboard and all implements there	15s
All vessels of wood and lumber goods	£1 5s
His clothworkers rack, his shears and all other implements used in his trade	
	£12

Total   £20 2s   6d

John Palmer	**Clothworker**	**1677-8**	**P2/P/513**

14 pair of shears and 30 corse of handles	£11 10s
2 pair of dubbing boards	10s
The rack and leads	£5
4 shear boards and brushes and pare boards	£2 10s
5 beds with the furniture	£5
One dozen of pewter, one furnace and 3 crocks, one kettle and other brass	
	£4 10s
One live pig	£1
For releasing of apprentice	£5
All other the instore and lumber goods	£1 10s

Total   £35 10s

Discharge

Paid for his funeral	£4
Paid to Mr Paul Methuen for cloth debt	£8
For charges at the visitation and horse hire and other expenses	£1
Pd John Hendrence for teasels	£2
	Total £15

Total net   £20 10s

Richard Dicke	**Clothworker 1682**	**P2/D/340**

18 pairs of clothworking shears and wearing apparel	£11 10s
3 shear boards, 3 paste boards and scrafe and two trestles	£2
6 brushes, 2 cutting boards and one form	16s
240 pounds of lead	£1 15s
40 corse of handles and stadges	£8
2 bubbing boards and 2 trestles	10s
One setting rack	£4
One setting press and 2 sets of papers	£11 10s
One rack and one jack	12s
4 kettles, one brass pan and one bell metal pot	£2 15s
2 spits, one small kettle pot and one warming pan	6s 6d
One dozen of pewter plates, 2 flagons and 3 candlesticks	£1 2s
11 pewter platters	£1 10s
5 pewter dishes	3s
One pair of andirons and dogs	4s
One fire pan and tongs	4s
One table board, 9 joined stools and one cupboard	£3
One chest of drawers, one chest, 2 boxes, one side board and 6 chairs	£2 7s
3 barrels, 2 tubs, one trendle and one tub	14s

Total   £54 4s 6d

Due on debts besides the aforesaid inventory the sum of £40 and upwards

Anthony Matthew   Clothworker 1691   P2/M/703

His wearing apparel and money in his pocket   £3

Inner Chamber

One bed and bedstead with its furniture and 6 chairs   £2

Outward Chamber

One bed and bedstead and the furniture, one trunk, a box and table linen

    £2   2s 6d

Hall

One chest and other furniture   6s 6d

Kitchen

6 small pewter dishes and other small pieces of pewter   10s 4d

2 brass pots and some other small brass vessels   9s 2d

One table board, one joined form, 2 joined stools   8s 3d

Buttery

7 barrels and other wooden vessels   £1 1s 6d

Brewhouse

One small boiler   10s 6d

Shop

21 pair of shears   £10 7s 4d

3 shearboards and leads belonging to them   £1 18s 6d

3 dubbing boards with trestle and perches belonging to them   15s 4d

42 course of handles and the stages   £4 1s

One pack of teasels, some odd staves   £1 10s 6d

One clothworkers rack   £2 1s 6d

One clothworkers press and papers   £13

2 beds and some lumber things belonging to the shop   £2 7s

2 pieces of cloth   £6

One small cottage being chattel   £18

For lumber goods and things forgotten and unseen   10s

In debts when received   £94 8s

Total   £157 7s 11d

BROADWEAVERS

John Chapman   (Trowle)   [Broadweaver]   P2/C/152

One table boards with a back board, 2 trestles and one form	4s
One cupboard with a cloth	5s
2 turns	1s 8d
One gridiron, 2 pair of pothooks, 2 hangells	2s
4 brass pans, 2 cauldrons	£1 10s
3 crocks, one posnet	15s
4 candlesticks, one chaffing dish, one flour pot	5s
9 platters, 8 pottingers, 4 saucers	13s 4d

The Chamber

2 bedsteads, 2 flock beds, 3 bolsters, 2 pair of blankets, 3 sheets, 4 coverlets	
	£1 18s

Chamber within the Hall

One bedstead, one bed, one blanket, one bolster	2s
One frying pan, one skimmer	1s 2d
2 trendles, one barrel	1s 4d

Shop

2 broad looms, one kypesie loom with their apparel and furniture	£3

His wearing apparel	10s

5 geese	2s 6d
4 hens and one cock	1s 8d
One pair of bellows	4d

Barton and field

2 kine	£4
The third of 3 acres and a half of dredge corn and oats	12s
The skarme and warping hair	3s
Old iron about the house	3s
2 stalls of beasts	3s 4d
20 cheese	6s 8d

Total £15 1s	

John Florence senior   Broadweaver   1619   P2/F/105

Hall

One joined table board and a joined form	4s
An old cupboard	1s
2 pair of hangells of iron	1s
One form and one stool	4d
One platter of pewter and a pottinger	1s 6d
Two turns or wheels	10d

Buttery

4 trendles and 3 pails	5s
2 table boards and stool and a form	1s
A wooden bowl and 2 dishes and a can	3d
A sieve and a winnower	2d
A wooden tub	1s

Chamber

2 bedsteads, 2 flock beds, 2 flock bolsters, 2 flock pillows, a pair of blankets, one coverlet and 3 coarse sheets	£1
3 coffers	4s
A table board and form	1s
3 brass kettles, one brass pot, 2 broaches, a pair of pot hooks	16s
One wooden candlestick	1d
For dwelling house	£2 10s
His wearing apparel	3s 4d

Total   £5 10s 6d

[Whereas there is a loom bequested unto two of the children of Thomas Fisher, the loom was sold unto the father of the said children in the life time of John Fisher the elder to relieve himself in his sickness and also was helped out of the poor box monthly for the space of 2 years.]

Thomas Swaine   **Broadweaver**   **1631**   **P/S/201**

Bedding	£1 10s
22 pounds of brass	19s
His wearing apparel	10s
One sheet and a pillow	2s
2 barrels and trendles and pails, the hangells and a pair of pothooks	7s
A cupboard and a board, two blankets and a form in the Hall	8s
Three pounds of pewter	£2 3s 4d

Loft

One chest	6s
One bedstead and three coffers and a chair	10s
The wood and planks	9s

Total	**£4 19s 4d**

Debts due to the testator

Philip Grant	£2 10s
Robert Kears	£1
Richard Dick and John Druce	£5 6s 1d
Total	**£8 16s 1d**

Debts owing by the testator

William Norris	£1 6s
William Chandler	£1 4s 10d
John Peare	£1 4s
Francis Yerbury widow	8s
Philip Grant	1s
John Tucker	10½d

Total	**£4 4s 8½d**

Richard Hilpes   **Broadweaver**   **1635**   **P1/H/211**

Hall

One table board and form	3s 4d
Old planks that made benches and a form	9d
One powdering tub, 2 old chairs, a stool and a stock	2s
4 small kettles, 2 skillets, 2 small pots and 2 brass pans	£1 10s
One broach, a gridiron, 2 pothooks, one hangell and a skimmer, a hatchet, one spade	2s 6d
A bellows, one frying pan, a stool, some dishes and spoons with other small things	2s 6d

Shop

An old broad loom with his furniture, 2 quilting turns, a spinning turn, one reel, an old cupboard, one chair, a tub	£1 10s
6 small barrels, 5 coffers, one chest, one box	13s 4d

Hall chamber

One livery bedstead with cord mat	5s
3 coverlets, 2 blankets, 2 old stools, 3 pillows, one bolster, one flock bed	£1 10s

Shop chamber

One timber bedstead and an old board bedstead, 2 coverlets, 2 blankets, one bolster, one bed	10s
2 small trendles, 2 tubs, one kive and some wood lumber, some certain boards	12s 4d
2 grist bags, one wool bag	2s
Pewter	13s 4d
One spice mortar	2s
The wood without doors	£1
All his wearing apparel	£2

Total   £11 6s 1d

John Doggett   Broadweaver Bradford   1643   P2/D/230

Hall

One table board and a joined form	8s
One joined cupboard	£1
One old chair stool and a joined stool	1s 6d

Buttery

3 brass kettles and one crock	£2
One other pot of brass	8s
8 platters and porringers, one flagon pot	13s 4d
2 tubs, 2 barrels, 2 pails with other small implements	7s
2 brass skillets, one half dozen of tin spoons, 3 small saucers, one brass candlestick and a pewter cup	3s
One hangell, one pothook, one broach, a fire pan, one pair of andirons and a small salt	5s

Inner Chamber

One table board and frame, 2 joined stools, 2 chairs	
One livery bedstead, one coffer, one chest, one box	£1 10s
One Bible and other small books	8s
2 flock beds, 3 coverlets, one pair of blankets, 2 mats, one bed cord, 2 coffers, 2 pillows	£2 10s
An old tub and 39 pounds of yarn in it	£2 12s
40 pounds of wool	£2
6 pounds of coarse wool	2s

Outward Chamber

A pair of scales, 3 tubs, earth vessels	1s 4d
A spinning turn and reel	1s
All his wearing apparel with divers linen and woollen was carried away by the King's army	(nil)
2 load of wood and 8 sacks of coal	£1
2 acres of beans, rye and wheat	£2 13s 4d
Debts owing on bond	£40
Total	**£58 12s 6d**

George Beverstock sen   (Bradford Leigh)   Broadweaver 1688
P2/B/1106

One score of sheep	£4 5s
4 pigs	£1 10s
3 heifers	£3 15s
5 kine	£11 5s
One stack of hay	15s
12 kine	£27
One rick of hay	£2
One rick of hay	£1 10s
One rick of hay	£4
9 calves	£2 15s

Hall

2 table boards, 2 forms, one cupboard, one great chair and one little chair	£1
2 cheese presses, 2 cheese tubs, 4 cheese vats, one mashing tub, one cooler, 3 round trendles and 2 churns	£2
2 barrels, 2 bowls and other lumber goods	6s

Cheese Loft

2 barrels	5s
Cheese	£4
Cheese racks and tacks and other lumber	10s

Middle Chamber

One bedstead with the bed and all appurtenances and one table board	15s

Hall Chamber

One standing bedstead with a bed and all thereunto belonging and one chest and 2 coffers and other lumber	£3

For goods in the shop	£1
Bacon	£3 12s

Middle Room

2 spinning turns, 3 little chairs, one pair of andirons and a firepan and tongs, one salt box, one stool, one pair of hangells	8s

Hall

4 pewter platters	5s
One pewter chamber pot and one flagon and one pewter cup	3s
One brass pan, 4 kettles, 2 warming pans, 3 kettle pots, and a skillet and a skimmer and a basting ladle	14s

Total   £76 13s

Anthony Deverell   Broadweaver   1697   P2/D/410

His woollen wearing apparel	£1	5s
His linen and sheets		5s

Shop

2 looms and one harness and those things thereunto belonging	£5	5s
The wood in the shop and coals in the chamber	4s	6d

Kitchen

Cupboard		3s
3 barrels		6s
A table board and 2 benches		8s
2 stools		1s
2 other stools and a little form		1s
A trencher rack and 6 trenchers		2s
A pair of dogs, fire pan and tongs	1s	6d
A pair of andirons, one spit and heater, a pair of hangells		3s
2 trendles and 2 pails		5s
A pair of bellows and 2 bowls, a salt box, 2 ranges and a coal grinder		2s
31½ pound of brass at 10d a pound	£1	6s
11 pounds of iron		1s
A bell metal bott, 15½ pounds a piece	5s	6d
34 pounds of pewter		£1
A warming pan and a basting ladle		3s
3 chairs		6d
Shelves		2s

6 napkins, one holland sheet, one pillow case, 3 cravats, 2 caps and a bolster case	10s

2 coffers   4s
An ordinary bed and bedstead and appurtenances in the first little chamber 10s
An ordinary bed and bedstead in the innermost little chamber   10s
A high turn and a lantern   1s 6d

Total £13 5s 6d

WEAVERS

John Davis   **Weaver**   **1590**   **P2/D/38**

Hall

One posnet, one skillet   2s 4d
One brand iron, a pair of hangells   8d
A pail   3d
A weigh beam and scales   1s 4d
4 instruments and books   8s

The Chamber

A bedstead   8d
A flock bed and a bolster   6s 8d
A pair of blankets   3s 4d
One coverlet   3s 4d
One coffer   1s 4d
One old cloak   1s

Eleven pounds of list yarn   2s
All his wearing apparel   15s
2 barrels   8d
2 wimbles and 2 chisels   4d
A graffing saw   2d

In the shop

One broad loom with the furniture   £2
One coverled harness   2s 4d
Two kersey looms with the furniture   £1 2s
A hatchet   4d

Money   £2 10s

Total £8 1s 9d

Anthony Lacy   **Weaver**   **1591**   **P2/L/54**

Hall

One table board, one form, one bench and one stained cloth	2s 6d
One cupboard, one chair and 3 stools	6s 8d
3 platters, one basin of pewter, 3 pottingers, 5 saucers, 3 flour pots, one pint pot	
4 spoons, 2 salt cellars	10s
One brass candlestick and one chaffing dish	2s 4d
2 brass pots, 2 brass pans, 3 kettles, one skillet, one skimmer	£1 13s 4d
2 hangells, 2 iron crocks, one pair of pot hooks, one frying pan, one brand iron, one broach, one chopping knife, one pair of bellows	2s
3 barrels, 2 standards, 2 kives, one powdering tub, one pail, one peck, one tankard, 6 wooden dishes, 2 trenchers and one ladle	6s

Uppermost Chamber

One standing bedstead with a stained tester, one feather bed, one bolster, one coverlet, 2 blankets	£1 6s 8d
One truckle bedstead with a little flock bed, 2 coverlets, one bolster and one blanket	10s
One little board, one pair of trestles, one flasket, 2 earthen crutches, one basket	

Lower Chamber

One joined bedstead with a stained tester, one flock bed, 2 coverlets, 2 bolsters and 2 pillows	£1 13s 4d
One joined square board with a cloth	3s 4d
3 coffers	4s
One tack board, one ring, one meal sieve, one broach	1s
5 yards of white cloth, 4 yards of red, 4 yards of black cotton	15s
His wearing apparel	16s
2 pairs of canvas sheets	8s
2 broad looms with all kinds of tackling	£4
2 quilting turns and one spooling turn	2s
One cock and one hen	1s
3 loads of wood	10s

                                                   Total   £13 14s 4d

Edward Doggett (Weaver) 1597 **P2/D/50**

One broad loom with all things belonging to the same	£1 6s 8d
3 platters, 4 pottingers, six saucers, and one salt cellar	6s
4 brass candlesticks, half a dozen spoons, one skimmer	2s
One cupboard and one board with a form	6s
3 barrels, 2 trendles, one cowl	4s
One spinning turn and a reel and a hatchet	1s
3 cauldrons, one crock, a frying pan and a skillet	3s 4d
One coffer and 2 boxes	2s
One malt sieve, a lantern, a weigh beam and scales and a stool	1s
One bed, one pair of blankets, one coverlet and a bolster	13s 4d
One bed, a pair of blankets, one coverlet and a bolster and a pillow	10s
3 sheets and a board cloth	6s
2 jerkins, one doublet, 2 pair of breeches, a cloak, a pair of stockings and two shirts	10s
3 bedsteads	3s

Total   £4 14s 4d

William Fisher **Weaver** 1603 **P2/F/66**

Hall

One table board and 2 forms	1s 4d
One coffer and 2 bowls	1s
One barrel, one pail	8d
One old vat, 2 stools, one spinning turn, one chair	1s 6d
One brass crock, one kettle, one posnet, one skimmer	10s
One dozen trenchers, half a dozen spoons, 6 dishes and a ladle	8d
One broad loom with all his furniture	£2

Chamber

One board bedstead with a flock bed, 2 flock bolsters, 4 blankets, 2 pair of sheets, 2 coverlets	£1 10s 8d
2 platters, 2 pottingers, one salt, 2 saucers	2s 6d
One ring, one malt sieve, one keed kiver	1s
One pair of hangells, one frying pan	8d

3 coffers	5s
One grater and one brush	3d
His wearing apparel	16s
John Weethy by debt	£1 8s
Thomas Fisher the younger by debt	10s
William Ponting by bond	£1 10s
John Nicholls	15s
In money	£9

Total £18 14s 3d

Isaac Watts	**Weaver**	**1622**	**P1/W/94**

Hall

One table board with a frame, one form with two joined stools with barrels
  and other wooden vessels   £1

The pewter in the same place   10s

The brass viz 2 crocks, 4 pans, 2 skillets with a brazen mortar and such like
  stuff   £1 10s

The Chambers over the Hall and Kitchen

Wool fifty weights   £45

8 bundles of fine yarn   £20

One standing bedstead with a truckle bed with bedding and coverlets and
  blankets to the same as also 3 chests, one little table board with other
  lumber   £2 13s 4d

Debts owing and in ready money within the house   £20

His wearing apparel   £5

A little barrel of oil   £1

Linen: 3 pairs of sheets, one pair of pillows with board clothes, napkins and
  towels   £1

The wood in the barton with the scales and other lumber   15s

The lease of the house   £5

Total   £103 8s 4d

Luke Stevens (Holt)   Weaver   1635   P2/S/513

Hall

One table board and benches, one form, 2 chairs and a little table, one tack,
one rack   £1
2 pair of hangells, one pair of pothooks, one pair of tongs, one pair of and
irons, one pair of bellows, 2 broaches, one frying pan, one dripping pan
10s

Little Chamber below

One little board, one coffer, one bedstead, one feather bed, one flock bed
one pair of tables   £1 10s

Chamber above

One feather bed, one flock bed, 2 bolsters, 2 pillows, 3 blankets, 3 coverlets,
one carpet, one press, one bedstead, one chair, 2 coffers, one trunk   £5

Other Chamber

One flock bed, 3 blankets, 2 coverlets, 2 bolsters, 2 pair of sheets, one linen
tester, 2 board clothes, 6 table napkins, 4 pillow cases, one bedstead, one
press, one board, one box, one coffer, one flasket, a weigh beam, scales and
weights, a beating hurdle, 2 joined stools   £3

Cheese Loft

One powdering tub, a cheese rack, cheese and apples   £2

White House

The brass and pewter   £3
A powdering tub and silt stone with other implements   £1 10s

3 kyne, one calf and the hay   £10
5 sheep   £1
One broadloom and tackling   £1 10s
One ground of pasture leasehold   £7
The wood   £1
The corn as wheat, barley and beans   £2
The poultry   3s
2 pigs   £2

A ring stone	1s 8d
2 stems of trees	5s
The wool	2s 6d
His wearing apparel	£1 10s

Total   £44 2s 2d

Henry Webb (Winsley) Weaver   1641   P2/W/427

A table board and two forms	13s 4d
2 chairs, 2 stools and an old form	4s
A frying pan, one hangell and a pair of bellows	2s 6d
2 kettles, one crock, one posnet, a pair of pothooks and a skimmer	

Buttery

3 platters, 5 saucers, 2 salts, a pewter bowl, and 2 candlesticks	7s 6d
2 barrels, one pail, one trendle, a butter churn and a cowl	7s
A cupboard, a broach, a ring, a timber bottle, a malt sieve, and a plank board	
	4s
6 dishes, 4 spoons, a bowl and a little spice mortar	3s
3 tacks, 3 tubs, a pair of shears with other lumber	4s 6d
Cheeses valued at	12s 4d

Chamber

All his wearing apparel	£2 10s
2 bedsteads, 2 flock beds, one bolster, 2 pillows, 3 coverlets, 2 blankets	
	£2 11s 8d
A chest, a coffer and two boxes	6s 8d
A sheet, a table cloth and 2 napkins	3s 4d
Wool valued at	13s 4d
7 loose boards	7s
A brush with other small implements	1s 8d

Shop

A broad loom and a quilling turn	£1 10s
Some loose boards with other lumber	8s

In the barn

All manner of grain	£6
Hay	£1 3s 4d
A spade, shovel, a nipper and a pike	1s 8d

In the backside

Wood	10s
One cow and a heifer	£3
24 sheep	£4
2 swine	£1 6s
	8d
Wheat in a rick	£1
Rick staddle stones	1s
One cock and 3 hens	1s 8d
Wheat in the field 2 acres	£1 3s 4d

Total	**£31 17s 6d**

Debts owed by the deceased while he lived:

William Foord	£5
John Kent, gent	£1 3s 6d

WORSTED COMBER

John Markes	**Worsted comber**	**1678**	**P2/M/582**

His wearing apparel	£3
One flock bed with the appurtenances	£3
2 kettles	£1 6s 8d
One brass pot and bell metal pot	£1
½ dozen pewter and a cup and flagon and chamber pot	£1
One barrel, 2 tubs, one pail	7s
One iron for clamps	2s
One flock bed and bedstead with appurtenances	18s
His little chest and great chest	16s
One bedstead and table board with one cupboard	£1 3s
2 chests and what is in them	10s
All the lumber in the shop and in the hall	8s
3 serges at £2 per serge	£6
86 pounds of wool at 6d a pound	£2 3s

3 boxes, one little trendle and a pail		5s
One little mashing tub, one dozen trenchers, one bell	2s	6d
One little broach and 2 chairs	1s	6d
One pair of wool combs and charcoal	8s	6d

Total   £22   11s   2d

CARDMAKER

Anthony Aste   **Cardmaker**   **1676**   **P2/A/263**

His wearing apparel   £3
In ready money   £16
Owed upon shop book   £14

Chamber over the all
One feather bed, one bedstead   with all bed clothes, bedding and
    appurtenances, one table board, one side board, one chest, four joined
    stools, one pair of andirons with one box an all other implements in the
    same chamber   £7   10s
All his linen   £2   5s

Chamber over the Shop
One bed, one bedstead with all the appurtenances and apparel and also on
    table board, one form, one coffer, 2 joined stools with all other implements
    there and in the little chamber there adjoining   £2   10s

Hall
His brass and pewter and all implements of iron   £4   10s
All other lumber goods and implements   £1   5s

Buttery
5 barrels and all other vessels of wood and lumber there   £1   10s

Cockloft
One bed, one bedstead and all bedding and bed clothes and all other
    implements there   £1   10s

All his stock or goods for his trade with his working implements   £3

Total   £57   5s

MERCERS, CHANDLERS, VINTNERS, INNHOLDERS

MERCERS

Adam Hillard   **Mercer**   **1630**   **P1/H/183**

Shop
The wares of all sorts   £63 11s 5d

Inner Chamber
One standing bedstead with one bed and its furniture with one truckle bed
                                                         £5 10s
One table board with joined stools, boxes, trunks and andirons   £2

The Middle Room
One great chest with two table boards, one sideboard, one chair   £1 8s

The Kitchen
All the pewter and brass   £8 17s 6d

Higher Loft
One bedstead, one side board with other implements   12s

Middle Higher Loft
One bedstead with one bed with its furniture and one truckle bed with its
   furniture, one chair   £3 6s
Sheets and pillowcases and table cloths with all other linen   £5 9s 4d

His wearing apparel with one bible and other books   £3
The lease of his house   £3
Debts due unto him as appears by his book   £26
Allowed for things forgotten   3s 4d

Total £122 17s 1d

William Audley senior   **Mercer**   **1633**   **P2/A/160**

Shop

14 yards of linsey woolsey	11s 8d
6 ells of canvas	6s 6d
3 ells and a half of canvas more	3s 2d
13 yards of fustian with some remnants	15s
More canvas 16 ells	15s 4d
5 ells and a half of cushion canvas	4s
12 ells of lockram	12s
19 ells and a half of Popes Minsters	5s
4 ells of Hamrow	2s 4d
23 yards of broad tack	£1 5s
4 yards and a half narrow tack	3s
13 yards and a half of say	16s 6d
9 yards and a half of calico	6s 9d
9 yards of blue linen	6s 9d
10 yards of brown sackcloth	10s
21 yards of sackcloth	10s 6d
One ell of brown holland	1s 6d
8 yards of tufted fustian	4s 8d
One ell and a half of dowlas and one remnant of holland	3s
3 yards of tufted holland	3s
8 yards of buckram	4s
6 ounces of silk	8s
The scales, boxes, pint and half pint with other small things	10s
12 pounds of currants	4s
14 pounds of raisins	2s 6d
2 gallons and a half of oil	10s
The pestle and mortar	15s
One oil pan with other things	3s
Half a bushel of salt	1s
2 shop chests	13s 4d
Oat meal	1s 4d
The silk lard pointes and other small things	£1 5s 2d
The ribonning, the dried fish and other things	£1 15s 9d
The stockings, garters and other small things	£2 1s 2d
In money in the shop	£1 7s 7d

Hall

One table board with the frame and form; one stool; 2 chairs one cupboard

£1

One rack, 2 andirons, one pair of tongs, one fire pan, one iron bar, one
   hangells, one pair of bellows with certain books   5s

2 cups, one basin and ewer, one cupboard cloth and one brass candle stick 5s

Buttery

4 barrels, 4 brass crocks, 4 skillets, 2 dripping pans, 2 basting ladles, one
   brass chaffing dish, 2 broaches, 2 pair of pothooks, with other lumber   £2

Cock Loft

2 brass pans, one kettle, one bedstead, one old board with other lumber   £1

Little Chamber

One chest, 12 platters, one flagon, 8 porringers, 11 saucers, 3 pewter
   candlesticks, 3 salts, one basin and 2 little turns   £1 15s

Inner Chamber

One standing bedstead, one truckle bedstead, 4 chests, one little table board,
   one drawing box and 2 tacks   £1 16s
One feather bed, 2 flock beds, 2 pair of blankets, 4 bolsters, 4 pillows,
   2 coverlets, one green rug and one sheet   £4 6s 4d
One pair of fine holland sheets, 3 table cloths, 5 pillow cases, 2 pair of dowlas
   sheets, 2 pair of canvas sheets, one cupboard cloth, one dozen and a half of
   table napkins, one bolster case, 2 hand towels, 2 little table cloths, 2 little
   drinking cloths, one pair more of canvas sheets and one lockram sheet
     £2 19s 8d

Broad Hall Chamber

One long table board with a joined frame, 6 stools, one chair   £1
One standing bedstead, one truckle bedstead, one cupboard, one cupboard
   cloth and 2 little stools   £1 15s
2 beds, one pair of blankets, 2 bolsters, one rug, one carpet and 6 cushions
     £2
7 silver spoons and one bowl tipped and footed with silver   £1 10s
One cupboard cloth and a brush and one pair of andirons   3s 4d

80

One coverlet	10s
His wearing apparel	£2 10s

Washing House
4 trendles, 3 cowls, one powdering tub, one chamber pot, one hammer, one
shovel, one black bill with other lumber   £1   5s

Stable
One salting trough, one load of wood with other lumber   8s

In ready money	£52 1s 6d
More in ready money	19s 6d

Total   £98 14s 6d

Michael Tidcombe   (Mercer)   1684   P2/T/337

Shop
6 pieces of cloth and 26 yds linsey   £2 8s
22 yds calico, 15yds coverlet linen, 19 yds fustian, one piece fustian and
remnant   £3 16s
26 yds blue lining, a remnant Bengali, 29 yds calico and linen, 13 ell holland
£2 14s 6d
46 yds buckram, calico and Hastan, 62 yds fustian buckram linen and striped
cloth   £2 15s
123 ell of coloured and canvas and coarse cloth   £3 15s 10d
One piece Hamborough cloth and 90 yds linen cloth and linsey   £5
One piece crocus , 58 yds of tick fustian and linen and Bengali   £2 11s
7 dozen and 2 pair of hose apparel remnants, 31 yds tick and linen £2 7s 6d
2 parcels remnants, 37 yds tick and 4 pieces of cambric   £5 17s
2 pieces of muslin remnant, a fine cambric, 2 ell of plashe and 8 ells of
holland, 10 yds of black sasnet   £9 11s
40 yds of serge and 31 yds of say   £9 12s
50 yds of gold and silver golom and 24 yds of silver lace and one parcel of
green silk lace   £5 16s 6d

30 gross of buttons and a parcel of thread and 18 books and 3 parcels of
sasnet   £7 13s 6d
12yds black lace, 13 yds sasnet   £1 16s
Copper lace, 2 parcels silk and 7 silk scaped jacks and lacing   £1 7s
140 yds of stutte and a parcel of remnants, 22 ell of canvas dowlas
                                                                £15 10s 6d
One frock and one pair of trousers and 5 yds camleat, 5 pieces of forret
ribbon and 24 yds forret and 8 pieces of cotton forret, 8 pieces of tape, one
parcel remnant and 8 pair and 7 pieces of golom   £21 10s
13 gross gem for button, 4 ½ ell of silk, 2 pieces Holland and 6 pieces of
canvas, thread and tape, book, pins and boxes, inkle tape and wax and
books and goods in them, 10 pair of bodices, one piece of dowlas and
3 parcels of dowlas caudle moudges and kupes, locks, twine nails and cards
                                                                £28 1s
4 remnants stuff and 3 pieces of fustian and a remnant, 12 yds one piece
Bengali, 36 coloured linen, 15 ell Holland, 36 yds tick, one piece of
coloured, 4 pieces of holland   £20 13s 6d
24 yds of swan skins and linen, 97 ell of dowlas, 34 ell of canvas, one piece of
striped linen, 156 ell of canvas more   £10 10s
Cloves, pepper and other spices, raisins and currants, 3 dozen boone and half
a hogshead of vinegar, a hogshead and a half of metheglin and one hogs
head honey,2 hogsheads tobacco, one cwt starch, 10 bushels of salt, 2 cwt
pitch   £38 14s

Warehouse

Chalk, ashes, soap and sugar and glue, hops, jugs and earthenware, besoms,
hemp and 8 dozen glasses, 24 ell of canvas and dowlas and fine thread and
6 pieces tape and 10 gross buttons   £31 9s

Best Chamber

One bedstead with another bed and bolster and feather pillow, one white rug
with a suite of curtains and valences, 4 leather chairs, one table board,
2 joined stools with a carpet, one set of drawers, one hanging cloth, one
basket, one dressing box, one pair of large andirons with fire pan and tongs,
and one pair of bellows, one dozen diaper napkins and table cloth, 7 pair of
sheets and other linen with lumber goods   £23 2s

Little Chamber

7 silver spoons, 2 small silver dishes, one kadell cup and other small toys
£3 2s

Shop Chamber

One bedstead with a feather bed and bolster and pillow and rug and one pair
of blankets, 2 trundle bedsteads and one flock bed and bolster and rug with
mat and cord and one suite of curtains and valences, one chest, 2 boxes,
one sideboard, one wool cushions, one pair of andirons, one stool with
other lumber goods
£12 4s

Stair Head

One trunk, one coffer, one box
10s

Kitchen

17 pewter platters, 2 dozen small pewter dishes and plates, 2 sisstells , 4 brass
crocks, 2 skillets, 4 leather chairs, 6 wooden chairs, a table board, 6 joined
stools, one pair of andirons, one pair of large dogs with fire pan and tongs,
one pair of bellows with other iron, lumber one warming pan, 2 spits with
other small lumber
£10 12s

Tobacco House

One engine and press and other lumber there belonging
£6

Warehouse

One press, 15 barrels and hogsheads, 3 tubs and 2 pails and the shop chest,
pestle and mortar and other lumber
£5 14s

One furnace and pair of andirons, one flock bed with several other lumber
goods
£3 4s

One great weigh beam with scales and weights belonging
£1

His wearing apparel with several other things thereto belonging
£6

Total goods
£309 16s 10d

Forth on the shop books in debts good and bad
£251 3s

Rest in cash
£44

Total   £604 19s 10d

CHANDLER

Henry Elliott   Chandler or soap boiler   1679   P2/E/194

Hall

2 small plates, 5 small pieces of pewter, one tankard all about 8 lb weight,
   one pair iron grates, fire pan and tongs, a pair of bellows,one spit, a pair
   of andirons, one steeling iron, 2 great old chairs, 3 smaller chairs, 2 candle
   sticks, some mugs and glasses and other small implements   £1 1s

Buttery

3 barrels, one tun dish, one sieve, one ring with other small implements   10s

Chamber over the Hall

One bedstead cord and mat, a round table, one small trunk, one little coffer,
   one old box, one chair and some small glasses   £1 4s

Chamber over the Entry and Shop

18 dozen of besoms, about 2 bushels of chalk, a press engine and boxes to
   the same   £3 10s

Inner Chamber over the Buttery

His wearing apparel viz one shirt and some old linen   £1

Backside and Warehouse

A furnace for making soap, a grate and ladle and other old material for the
   same, the stones, troughs and ashes and soil   £8 10s

Shop

3 cwt of oil soap and 3 dozen and half of ordinary about 14 dozen one cwt
   and ½ of tallow and 8 dozen and quarter of candles   £15 1s
½ cwt and 24 lb glue, earthenware, prissons , bears and bottles, glasses and
   mugs, 5 lampblack barrels 1 whesker and 3 doz tuckers, 2 ream of brown
   paper and 12 lb cork and corks, 15 quire of white paper   £3 1s 8d
In leaf tobacco and growings and 30 lb cut, 4 bushels salt, one gall vinegar, 14
   lb molasses, 4 lb starch and some blue   £3 15s 6d
27 brushes of several sorts, fruit and spices and sugar and some seeds,
   14 lb of coloured and brown thread, 9 pieces inkle   £5 3s 10d

11000 pins, 14 tin boxes, 3 pieces and half of tapes, 3 doz cadic, 10 doz
  cottons, One doz ½ girdling Welch inkle thread and leather poyds and laces
  £1 12s 9d
9 primers , 7 lb powder and barrel, 3 sets of boxes, 7 other boxes, 12 barrels
  and casks and 2 great tubs an (--) mortar   £1 8s 6d
A window grate, 4 pair small scales, one great beam and scale, some small
  weights and about ½ cwt lead   £1 5s
3 old chests, a small reel, a pair of horse pots, and a bag and some other
  small implements   15s
Money in the house 22s, £10 in good debts about £10 more in very bad and
  desperate debts   £11 2s

Total   £59 1s 3d

VINTNER

Robert Phipp   **Vintner**   **1605**   **P2/P/152**

Hall

One table board with a frame, one cupboard, one wainscot chair, 3 stocks and
  one jack to hold a basin upon   10s

Parlour

One long table board with a frame and a form, one bench, the wainscot under
  the window, 12 joined stools with one little stool, a chair and one court
  cupboard   £1
Two great standing bedsteads with a truckle bed, one large cupboard of wain
  scot and one settle   £5
Two flock beds, two bolsters, two pairs of pillows, two pairs of blankets and
  2 coverlets, one dornick the other of green rug   £3 6s 8d
In the press, 2 coverlets, 2 carpets, 2 cupboard cloths, one sideboard cloth
  and 12 cushions   £3 13s 4d
2 curtains for the window and a curtain rod   6s 8d

Chamber over the Parlour

One table board with three forms, one standing bedstead and a settle
  £1 6s 8d

One flock bed, one bolster, one pair of blankets, one pair of pillows and one
  coverlet   £1 10s

Chamber over the Hall
One table board with 2 trestles, one form, one standing bedstead   6s 8d
One flock bed, one bolster, one pillow, 2 blankets, 2 coverlets   £1

Chamber over the Kitchen
One table board with a frame, 2 forms and one field bedstead   6s 8d
One flock bed, one bolster, one pillow, one pair of blankets and one rug   £1

Chamber over the Entry
One table board with a little bedstead, one flock bed, one bolster, one pair of
  blankets and an old coverlet   13s 4d

Chamber over the Cellar
A small parcel of wool with certain old lumber, one tub and such like   £1

Chamber over the Buttery
One table board, one form, one bedstead with a truckle bed, 3 coffers, 2 pair
  of playing tables   (---)
2 flock beds, 2 bolsters, one pair of pillows, 2 pair of blankets, 3 coverlets
                                                                           (---)

Inner Chamber
One table board with a from, 3 chests, one wainscot box, one large press with
  a wainscot bedstead   £3
One flock bed, 2 bolsters, one pair of pillows, one pair of blankets and
  one white coverlet   £1 13s 4d

Linen
18 pair of sheets   £7
22 table cloths   £4
5 dozen table napkins   £1 13s 6d
30 towels   £1
12 pillow cases   £1

His wearing apparel
2 hats, 3 jerkins, 3 doublets, 4 breeches, 4 pair of stockings, one cloak,
   6 shirts, 6 bands, 6 handkerchiefs, 3 night caps   £5

Plate
4 goblets whereof 2 are parcel gilt, one with gilt the other white   £5

Pewter
4 basins and one ewer, 2 pie plates, 2 dozen platters of all sorts, 4 dozen of
   plate trenchers, 10 saucers, 9 potage dishes, 17 pots great and small, one
   nest of pewter cups with 4 more of another sort, 4 dozen tin spoons, 7
   chamber pots, 3 pewter candlesticks, 4 flour pots   £3

2 pairs of bellows, one (----), 2 treen platters, one (---) of ladles,
12 wooden dishes, one bar [document corrupted]   (---)

Buttery
One safe, 3 brewing vessels, 10 barrels, 5 dozen trenchers, 3 pails, 20 stone
   jugs, one dozen glasses, one tun dish, 2 flaskets, 3 sieves, 4 sacks   £2

Barton
The fennel by estimation 12 loads   £3
The boar's sty, two stone trough, 2 boytling stocks, 2 forms, 3 planks 5s
   4 swine   £1 6s 8d

The Shop
One bucking cowl, a rinsing tub, 8 wine barrels, 2 hogsheads, 2 pipes, the
   wine, a partition, certain tacks and the horses   £2

Stables
The manger and the racks   5s

Debts owing to him
John Dowdings   £1
The church   £1 4s

Total   £69 3s 4d

INNHOLDERS

Robert Townsend   Innholder   1630   **P2/T/152**

Hall
One table board and frame and one form, one cupboard and one chair   10s

Parlour
2 bedsteads with one feather bed, one flock bed with the furniture to the
same, one table board and one form with 3 joined stools and one cupboard
and one sideboard and one chest and one chair, one carpet and 6 cushions
with other lumber   £10

Kitchen
One furnace, 3 brass pots, 3 spits, one dripping pan, one skillet, 2 cauldrons,
one colander, 2 kettles, one mashing vat, 3 pairs of hangells, 2 pairs of
pothook, one gridiron, 2 pair of iron andirons, fire shovel and tongs with
other lumber   £4

Wine Cellar
One hogshead containing 8 gallons of sack, another hogshead containing in
the same 12 gallons of claret and one little runlet containing 4 gallons of
white wine, one dozen and a half of pewter, 4 pewter candlesticks, 2 pewter
salt cellars, one pewter plate, 3 pewter chamber pots, one pottle pot, 3
quart pots, 3 pint pots, one dozen saucers and a dozen spoons of pewter
with other lumber   £3 10s

Beer Cellar
8 hogsheads and 2 kives with other lumber   £1

Chamber over the Entry
One high bedstead with one feather bed, one flock bed and one trundle bed
and the furniture thereto belonging, one table board, one form, one side
board and a carpet thereon with a basin and ewer, one coffer, 2 chairs and 4
joined stools with one warming pan and 2 dogs   £4

Chamber over the Beer Cellar
One table board and frame and 2 forms, one press, one high bedstead and

one low bedstead with 2 flock beds and the furniture to the same belonging, one chest and 2 small boxes £3

Chamber over the Parlour

One high bedstead with one feather bed with the furniture for the same, one table board, one form, one chair £2 2s

Chamber over the Hall

One low bedstead, one flock bed with the furniture to the same and one table board with 2 forms with other lumber £1 6s 8d

Chamber over the Kitchen

One field bedstead and one flock bed with the furniture to the same. One table board and 2 forms £1 5s

One other Chamber adjoining to the Chamber over the Kitchen

One low bedstead with a flock bed and the furniture to the same 15s

Linen: 6 pairs of sheets, one dozen and a half of napkins, 3 pair of pillow cases, 3 table board cloths, 3 towels £15

2 wine bowls of silver, one of them being gilt £4

His wearing apparel £6 13s 4d

One dun mare and 6 pigs £5

Wood in the backside £2

Hay in the haymow and in the backside £6 13s 4d

Outward Room

2 table boards and 2 forms 5s

Total   £62 0s 4d

Moneys owing to diverse persons at the time of his death £117 11s

Edward Dick   **Innholder**   **1668**   **P1/D/121**

Hall

2 table boards, 3 joined stools, 2 old forms, one cupboard, 2 chairs   £1 10s
5 broaches, one spit, one pair andirons, one pair old coal grates, one fire pan
   and tongs, 2 hangells, one jack, 2 pothooks, warming pan and all other
   implements there   £1 18s
91 lbs pewter at 9d a lb   £3 8s 3d
One great brass pot   £1 10s
In crock brass and skillets with the kettle or cauldron 56 lb at 6d a lb   £1 8s
Basting ladle, skimmer and spoons   4s
2 bascrells and all other implements and lumber   6s

Brewery

2 furnaces with their appurtenances   £2 10s
All the brewing vessels and implements there   £1

Chamber over the Brewhouse

One bedstead, one bed and all other implements and lumber there   £1

Backside

A bucket and chain and the lumber there   3s

Cellar

2 hogsheads of beer   £1
The hogsheads, barrels and all other lumber   £1

Chamber over the Hall

One press cupboard, 2 table boards, 3 forms, 10 joined stools, 2 chests, one
   sideboard, 2 boxes   £3 9s 6d
A pair of andirons, a pair of dogs, a fire grate and tongs and 3 chairs 12s
One feather bed, 3 flock beds, 2 bolsters   £4 5s
2 bedsteads with mats and cords, 2 rugs, 2 carpet cloths   £1 11s

Cockloft Chamber

2 bedsteads, 2 little flock beds, one bolster, one pillow, a pair of blankets,
   one rug   £1 15s

One chest, one coffer, one little table board, one joined stool, one box	17s
2 pair of sheets and all other linen	£1
2 more chests, one coffer, one little table board, 2 bedsteads with all other lumber	£1 7s
One flock bed, 2 rugs, 4 blankets with all other lumber	£1 6s
His wearing apparel	£1
One chattel hold estate determinable upon 2 of the lives of his children	£40
2 old bedsteads and a chest	15s

Total   £74 5s 9d

TRADES

TANNER

| **Robert Whatly** | **Tanner** | **1666** | **P2/W/491** |

His wearing apparel £1

One bedstead , 2 flock beds, a coverlet, a pair of sheets, 2 pillows, a bolster
and other implements £2 10s

His brass, pewter and other implements £2 10s

One chest, 2 coffers, 3 boxes, a chair and other implements £1

21 hides almost brought to perfect leather £10

52 green hides £15 19s 2d

5 dry hides of leather £2 16s

3 white hides 10s

14 dozen and a half of dry tanned calfskins £7 10s

8 dozen and 5 calf skins in the tan pits £2 15s

All his bark £8

All his tools and implements 2s

One horse beast with his saddle and furniture £1 10s

Owing him upon book of which we judge one third part to be desperate debt
£12

Total   £67   3s   2d

COOPERS

| **John Orpen senior** | **Cooper** | **1684** | **P2/O/53** |

Backside

200 hogshead staves £1

200 half hogshead staves 12s

100 small barrel staves 4s

16 dozen barrel heading £2 14s

5 dozen small bottoming 5s

250 kilderkin staves 15s

200 kilderkin staves 12s

400 of Rowle timber £1

1000 pail staves £1 10s

4 dozen of middle pieces	10s
200 pail staves	6s
8 dozen of small bottoming	12s
4 dozen of small bottoming	6s 8d
50 kilderkin staves	2s 6d
4 dozen bottoming	8s
1000 trendle timber	£1 10s
100 bottoming	12s
200 bottoming	£1
400 trendle timber	10s
5 dozen bottoms at 10s and 20 dozen at 40s	£2 10s
6 dozen bottoms at 9s, 100 pail staves at 7s	12s
500 cowl staves	£1
200 cowl staves	6s
15 dozen bottoming at 18d a dozen	£1 2s 6d
200 pail staves	5s
21 dozen hoops	£2 2s
40 dozen hoops	£2
24 dozen hoops	£1 4s
One brewing tub, 3 barrels, 3 pails, one turn	£1
750 elm boards	£3 7s
Old planks, trestles, lugs and forks	£1 10s
86 foot of board at 13s per 100	10s
400 foot of board at 13s per 100	£2 12s
100 at 10s	10s
200 at 20s and 60 foot of oak planks at 20s per 100	£1 12s 6d
His wearing apparel	£2
One bedstead, one bed with the furniture	£1 10s

Outer Chamber

2 bedsteads, 2 beds with the furniture	£1 10s
One great chest, table board, kiver and other lumber goods	£1
One great brass kettle, 6 brass pots, skillets and skimmer	£2
One dozen pewter dishes, one dozen pewter plates, 2 chamber pots, 4 candlesticks, 2 flagons, 2 pewter cups, 4 dishes	£2
One table board, settle, cupboard and other lumber goods	£1
Rough timber	£20
Book debts	£12

Total   £81 17s 8d

Henry Shrapnell   **Cooper**   **1688**   **P2/S/949**

Hall
Brass and pewter   £7 9s 2d
A table board, stools and other lumber   £3

Parlour
6 leather chairs, a table board and other lumber   £3

Kitchen
A furnace, a jack, 2 dripping pans, 2 fender andirons and other goods   £4
Wooden goods   £1

Hall Chamber
A bed and bedstead and all furniture   £7
6 chairs, a table board and other goods   £2 10s
Plate   £14

Parlour Chamber
One bed and appurtenances and other lumber   £3 10s

Garret
2 beds and all appurtenances and other lumber   £5

Buttery
Wood vessels with provision in house of bread, beer and the like   £5

Timber and timber goods   £40

The ground called Puddox   £20
Iron goods   £27
Wheat on the ground   £3

His wearing apparel   £10

In debts owed him on book   £65
In money in house   £37
In money at interest   £173

Total   £430 9s 2d

94

MALTMAN

Thomas Long   **Maltman**   **1600**   **P2/L/85**

Parlour

One table board, one form, 3 stools, one chair, 2 cupboards, a pair of and irons	13s
The pewter in the parlour	12s
One mortar, one brush	1s

The Entry Chamber

One old flock bed, one bedstead, one bolster, one pair of blankets, one coverlet	13s 4d
4 tubs, one trendle, one bushel, one peck, one garner, 6 bushels of barley	16s
6 sacks, one winnowing sheet	7s

Hall

One table board, one form, one spinning turn, one beating hurdle, 2 tacks, one salt tub	5s
One pair of scales	3s 8d
Wool and yarn	3s
One pair of tongs, one hangell	1s

Kitchen

2 brass pans, 2 kettles, 2 crocks, 2 skillets, one chaffing dish, one dripping pan, 2 spits, one malt mill, one spinning turn, 3 pails, one little board, one form, one brass ladle, one cheese press, one pitch pan and print mark 5 borers, one hatchet, one axe, one bill	£1 13s 4d
One handsaw, one hook	8s

Buttery

4 barrels, 2 salt tubs, 3 bottles, one cleaver, one wimble, one tun dish	2s
One brandiron, 1 (---)	2s

Inner Chamber

One joined bedstead, one truckle bedstead, one flock bed, one pair of blankets, 2 coverlets, one bolster, 2 pillows	£1 19s

His wearing apparel £2

One coffer, 4 pairs of sheets, 3 board cloths, 6 table napkins, 2 towels,
one other table cloth £2 1s 8d

2 bushels of wheat 6s

Cheese 5s 6d

Middle Chamber

One old bedstead, 2 flock beds, one bolster, one pair of blankets, one coverlet,
one press, 3 yards of cloth £2 3s 2d

Chamber over the Entry

One bedstead, one flock bed with a coverlet, 2 pillows, 2 pairs of towels,
one pair of blankets, 2 coverlets, 2 mats 3s 2d

One flasket, one malt sieve 12s

20 bushels of malt £2 10s

One rene of leather, one kype, one hand pannier, one reel 4s 1d

2 planks, one shovel 1s

One little board 6d

Chamber over the Parlour

2 cheese racks, one hundred cheeses, one churn, one board, one form, one
pair of stock cards £1 3s

Malt House

2 quarters of malt £2

3 ladders 2s

One scythe, one cutting knife, one cradle, 4 rakes, one fork, 3 weed hooks 2s

Stable

One mare £3

One hacking saddle, one pack saddle, one pike, 2 tamys ,one1 girth and bridle
6s 6d

One dust tub, one pair of hods, one fanure , one shepherd's crook, a bar box,
one short ladder 3s

Over the stable, 4 loads of hay £4

Backside

7 pigs	16s
Wood	£5 10s
3 kine	£5 6s 8d
2 yearlings	£1 10s
5 young cattle	£7 6s 8d
3 colts	£5 6s 8d
More in hay in the stall	£5
Plough harness	£3 6s 8d
3 hurdles	3s 4d
Ready money	£1

Debts due to the deceased

Thomas Marchant of Hilperton	7s
George Lovell	£1 1s
Richard Horn	£2

Debts owed

Richard Horn	£1 2s
John Holton	£1 2s
Mr Read	£7 10s
Besides various debts yet unpaid	

Total   £195 18s 2d

GLOVER

Robert Powell   **Glover**   **1610**   **P30/142**

Chamber

One flock bed, one bolster, 2 little feather pillows with the bedstead, 2 old
coverlets, 2 blankets and one pair of sheets   £1

2 old coffers, one old safe and 3 pieces of board   2s

One dozen and a half of penny purses, one dozen and a half of gloves with
the leather   13s 4d

His brush, the old paring knife, a beam, a knife, a withe, a stake, a pair of
shears, a mallet and sticks and small chisels   2s 6d

A kive, a little tub, an old cowl with the old treen vessels, a ladle with the
dishes, trenchers and 4 spoons   5s

2 old saddles, an old bridle, an old hatchet with old beam and scales   2s

An old crock, an old posnet, a skillet, a chaffing dish, a broach, a fire pan, a
frying pan, 2 dogs, a skimmer, a pair of hangells, a pothook, an old kettle
      10s

The pewter, 2 little candlesticks, a socket   2s

A square board, a furnace, a cradle, an old barrel, a pot lid and a stool   2s

Total   £2   18s   10d

CORDWAINER

William Coleman   Cordwainer   1693   **P2/C/829**

Divers pans of pewter weighing 64 pounds at 6d a pound	£1 12s
11 hogsheads and one half hogshead	£1 16s 6d
In wooden vessels	14s
One frying pan	6d
10 joined stools	10s
9 chairs	3s
One jack for roasting meat	5s
One pair of andirons and five dogs	6s
One broach, one fire pan, one tongs, one pair of hangells	2s 6d
One bacon rack	5s
A pair of fire grates with the appurtenances	10s
One settle	1s
2 chests, one box	10s
A chest of drawers	12s
One pair of andirons with brass heads with fire pan and tongs	5s
4 tables with their frames	10s
5 flock beds and bedsteads with coverlets and rugs, blankets, bolsters and pillows and all other appurtenances	£7
7 pair of sheets	£1
2 brass pots, one warming pan	8s
One brass skimmer	4d
2 furnaces and one boiler	£3 10s
One pump	£1 15s
	£21 15s 10d
Debts on book and otherwise but most desperate	£10 10s
Total	**£32 5s 10d**

SMITHS

John Godsell   **Smith**   **1598**   **P2/G/96**

Hall

| One round table board, a cupboard joined together and one joined stool | 3s | 4d |

One round table board, a cupboard joined together and one joined stool 3s 4d
One chair, 2 stools, one broach, 2 brass candlesticks, one chaffing dish 2s 6d
3 platters, 2 pottingers, 4 saucers, one salt cellar   1s 8d

Parlour

One low joined bedstead with a flock bed, 2 white coverlets, a bolster and one
  pillow   13s 4d
[Document corrupted] one great chest, 3 (---) and one little form   (---)
 One other bedstead (---) , (---) flock (---)   10s
(---) with (---) bed, one coverlet, one bolster   6s 8d
1 cupboard, 3 platters, 3 pottingers, 2 tin cups, onesalt and one candlestick 5s
2 coffers, one chair of elm, one hamper   3s
One coverlet and 3 pillows   5s
5 sheets, 2 holland pillows, 2 drinking cloths, 3 pillowcases, 3 table napkins
                                                                           £1 10s

Shop

3 brass crocks, 3 brass kettles, 5 little skillets and one posnet   £1
One horse to set drink and 3 barrels, 3 pails, 2 trendles and other old treen
  vessels   5s
2 platters, one tin cup, one frying pan, one turn, one reel   2s
One bedstead and one coverlet   2s 6d
His wearing apparel   £1 16s 8d
One lease of a Rowles ground of five acres

Total   £6   16s   8d

William Howell   **Blacksmith**   **1605**   **P1/H/32**

Hall

One table board with a frame, one joined form, three benches, one tack,
   one chair, one joined stool   5s
One andiron, one pair of hangells, one fire pan, one pair of tongs   1s 4d

Kitchen

4 brass pans, one cauldron, 3 crocks, one posnet, one skillet   £2 3s 4d
One brandiron, one frying pan, one brass chaffing dish, 2 broaches, one
   skimmer   3s 4d
One table board with a frame, one form, 2 tacks, 2 vats, one plank   3s 4d
2 pails, one trendle, one churn, one shovel, one hatchet, one bill, one tankard,
   one pair of bellows   2s 4d

Little House

4 barrels, 3 silts, 3 tacks, 3 cheese vats, one pair of butter scales and one
   pound stone   4s

Chamber over the Kitchen

One bedstead, one garner, 2 turns, one reel, 2 cowls, one bushel, one peck,
   one sieve   10s

Shop

One pair of bellows, one anvil, one bickhorn, one vice, one iron mortar and
   pestle, 2 sledges, 2 hammers, 3 pair of tongs, 2 pair of pincers, one stone
   trough with other small Implements   £1

Chamber over the Hall

One table board, 2 trestles, one form, 2 benches, one cupboard, one cheese
   rack   10s

Little Buttery

2 tacks, 2 dozen pewter, 3 tin bottles, 3 candlesticks, 3 tin cups, one dozen
   spoons, one dozen trencher , 3 wooden dishes, one ladle, one bowl   £1
2 silver spoons   4s

Chamber over the Shop

2 standing bedsteads, one truckle bedstead, one chest, 2 coffers	£1 10s
3 flock beds, 3 coverlets, one pair of blankets, 2 bolsters, one pillow	£2
3 canvas sheets, one pair of lockram sheets, 3 holland sheets, 2 pillow cases, 2 board cloths, one table napkin, 2 holland towels	£1 10s
4 books	2s
His wearing apparel	£1

Backside

One yetting stone, one grindstone, one cheese ring	10s

Corn and cattle

One load of wheat and one load of vetches	£1
3 kine	£5
3 heifers	£4
3 yearlings	£2
3 pigs	10s

Total   £24 8s 8d

James Watts   Blacksmith   1685   P2/W/662

Cockloft

5 dozen rakes, a sword and tuck, an old bedstead and some old iron and some
　other old small things   11s

Room under

A half headed bedstead, cord and mat, a flock bed and bolster and case,
　blanket, a sheet, a rug, a coffer, an old box, form and old stool   £1 6s 8d
A cupboard, a table board, 2 barrels and horse, glass bottles and earthenware,
　one candlestick and tinder box, an old fire pan and tongs, other small things
　 16s

Shop

13 clifts and pritchells, tools and wedges   4s
4 pair of tongs, 2 sledges, 4 hammers   12s
1 anvil and beckhorn   £3 16s
2 old vices, 7 files and small tools   12s
2 grinding stones and harness   16s
One old bellows, cole draw and blocks and other old lumber   14s 8d
48 bars and pieces of new iron 7cwt 2qr 7lb   £6 1s
Hooks and twist, jemells and plates 2qr   14s
Old iron   1cwt 2qr   14s
Edge tools and steel 1qr 7lb   11s 8d
In debts most of which very bad   £1 7s

Total   £20

John Moxham   **Blacksmith**   **1692**   **P2/M/720**

His wearing apparel   £4

Kitchen

A clock and case   £2 10s

A yard and weights   10s

8 pewter dishes, one dozen pewter plates, 3 porringers, one pewter tankard and one pewter candlestick   £2

2 brass skillets, 2 bell metal pots, a little brass pot, a brass kettle, one warming pan, one saucepan, one kettle, one basting ladle and one bell metal mortar and pestle   £2

One pair of grates, one pair of andirons, one fire pan and tongs, one dripping pan, 3 iron candlesticks, one frying pan, pair of hangells, 2 spits and some other ironware   £1 15s

One cupboard, one trencher rack with trenchers, one table board and frame, one settle, one bacon rack, 2 chairs and some other lumber goods   £2 3s

Cellar

5 half hogsheads and 3 other barrels, 2 barrel horses, one powdering tub, one salt, one brewing vat, 4 pails, one trendle, one mashing tub, 2 other tubs and other lumber goods   £2 10s

One musket, one birding piece, barrel and lord   16s

Kitchen Chamber

One bedstead, one feather bed and bedding with curtains and valence   £5

6 leather chairs, 6 joined stools, one cradle, one chest, one trunk, 3 boxes, one pair of dogs and one fire pan and tongs   £2 12s

One other bedstead, flock bed, rug and other bedding   £2

One dozen diaper napkins, one diaper table cloth, 3 pairs of sheets and other linen   £2

One table board   15s

Outer Garret

One bed and bedstead with bedding   £1 10s

Inner Garret

11 walnut planks	£1 7s 6d
One tester bedstead with a cord and mat	14s
One coffer	3s

Shop

All sorts of ironware and other goods	£55
Some ironware and all sorts of smithery tools	£15
Debts due on bond	£50
Debts due on books	£110
One house held on lease of 1000 years	£60

Total   £324 5s 6d

CARPENTER

Henry Painter   Carpenter   1594   P2/P/102

Parlour

One joined table board with a frame, one form, 2 benches and one back board	5s
One joined bedstead with a flock bed, one bolster, 2 blankets, 2 coverlets and 2 pillows	£1 10s 2d
One cupboard , one trippet of the bed, one coffer	10s
One old cupboard, one stool, 2 tacks	4s 4d
One carpet cloth	5s
2 hangells	8d
His wearing apparel	7s

Chamber over the Milhouse

One bedstead with a flock bed, one bolster, 2 blankets, one coverlet	10s
One bedstead, one kipe and a cheese rack	3s 6d
A chest with ears of corn in it	10s
A frail with hops in it	10d
One little form and 2 planks	9d
14 bushels of malt	£1 8s
5 joists of timber	2s 6d

Chamber over the Parlour

One bedstead with a flock bed, one bolster, 2 blankets, one coverlet and a
   tester 14s
2 coffers, one kipe, one ring, one broach, 3 locks · 3s 6d
One pick, one crook and old dagger · 8d
2 canvas sheets, one lockram sheet 3 board cloths, 3 pillows, one feather
   pillow · £1 1s
2 axes, 2 hatchets, 4 spoke shaves, 2 tenon saws, 2 hand saws, 6 chisels,
7 borers, 2 wimbles, 2 mallets, 6 planes, 2 compasses, 3 squares, 2 hammers
   12s
2 forms, one candle mould, one iron rake, one old saddle, one rip hook 3s 3d

Lower House

One table plank, one form, one bench · 3s
4 pillows, one table board, one form and one bench · 5s
2 kipes, 4 malt sieves · £1
One ring, one search, one quarter of wood · 1s
One spinning turn, one reel, 2 shovels · 2s

Buttery

One horse, 5 barrels · 5s
2 trendles, 2 vats, 2 kipes · 4s 8d
2 cauldrons, 3 crocks · £1 4s
One skillet, one ladle, one grid iron, one brand iron, one skimmer, 2 broaches,
   2 hangells, one pair of pothooks · 4s 10d
3 platters, 5 pottingers, 8 saucers, 4 salts, 2 candlesticks, one chamber pot
   9s 6d

Milhouse

A malt mill and a silt stone · 10s
3 sacks and a winnowing sheet · 3s
One bushel, one peck, one half peck, one strike · 1s 8d
One coop and 2 planks · 2s
2 pair of wain wheels · £1 6s 8d
2 pair of cart wheels · £1
3 wheels half made · 15s
One hundred of board · 4s 8d
2 planks and 2 drays · 1s 6d

106

Workhouse

11 cart stocks	11s
9 yokes and 50 felloes	£1
2 ladders	5s
8 pair of trestles, lugs and fork	2s 6d
3 planks and 3 plocks	3s

Kitchen

3 score felloes	£1
13 dozen spokes	13s
One yetting stone	10s
The bucket and chain and the windlass of the well	2s
A neast hurdle, one reel and one little kettle	2s
10 dishes, one dozen and a half of spoons and 2 dozen and a half of trenchers	1s 6d

Backside

A grindstone and a trough	12s
In wood	£1 6s 8d
One sheep	5s 4d
One stall of bees	2s 6d
One sow	10s
The timber	18s

All his debts	£2 11s

Total £27 17s 4d

MASON

| **Thomas Hunt** | **Mason** | **1612** | **P2/H/297** |

Oriel
One table board, one joined stool, one livery table with 3 yards of wainscot
and benches to the table piece   10s

Hall
One press, one table board, one form, one bench, one chair, one pair of
hangells   10s

Buttery
3 barrels with a bench for the same   5s

Under the stairs
2 kettles, 2 skillets, one bowl, one dough trendle, one tun dish, one ring, one
frying pan, one broach, one hatchet, one spade, with all his working tools
                                                                  15s

Chamber
2 beds, 2 bedsteads, 3 coverlets, 2 pair of blankets, 2 bolsters, one pillow,
2 pillow cases, one pair of sheets, 3 coffers, one board, half a dozen of
pewter, 2 pewter candlesticks, 2 salts, one turn, one pewter dish, half a
dozen spoons, one treen platter, one brush, one peppercorn, one chair,
one stool, one pewter tun dish, 2 bed mats   £3 10s

Loft
2 weight and a half of wool, 15 cheeses, 2 vats, one turn, one search, one
sideboard, one stool, 4 lead weights, one sheep's pent   £2 10s

Backside
One pile of wood   £1 13s 4d
15 hurdles   3s 4d

His wearing apparel   £2
49 sheep   £10 13s 4d

                                                    Total   £23 10s

Debts owing by Hunt

John Grace	£5
Upon a bond to Edward Long	£3 6s
Richard Horn	18s
Roger Deverell	8s
Robert Parish	4s 8d
Mrs Blanchard	4s
John Ivyleaf	2s
Tobias Love	3s 4d

Total   £10 6s

WIRE DRAWER

Jasper Drewett   Wire drawer   1681   P2/D/336

His wearing apparel, linen, woollen , stockings, shoes, boots,etc   £2

Hall

One dozen pewter cont. 30 lbs weight and 15 small pieces, 4 old kettles, one
brass pan, 3 small pots, one brass skillet, one skimmer, a basting ladle,
2 spits, one pair small andirons, a toasting iron, one pair pothooks, an old
wood jack, one settle, 2 chairs, a table board, form and old bench,
2 trencher racks and trenchers, an old dresser and shelves and several small
old implements   £4

Buttery

2 barrels, one old powdering tub, a small horse for barrels, 8 small pieces of
pewter, an old dresser, 3 shelves, a search and ring, earthenware and some
glasses and old implements   12s 6d

Kitchen

One brass pot, one skimmer, one brass candlestick, 2 pewter salts, an old
cupboard, 3 pair of pothooks, one pair dogs, one small trencher rack and
some trenchers, one fire pan and tongs, one pair bellows, 2 wire candle
sticks, a bacon rack, about one flitch of bacon, 2 frying pans, one old tub,
one old trendle, 2 old chairs, one joined stool, an old sideboard, one Bible
with some old lumber   £1 4s

Shop

About one bundle of wire, several old working tools, benches, grindstone and lantern   £2 13s 4d

Chamber

One tester bedstead, cord and mat, one half headed bedstead, cord and mat, 2 flock beds, 2 flock bolsters and cases, 6 pillows, one green rug, 3 old coverlets, one old under flock bed, 2 pair of blankets, 2 pair of sheet and one old pair, 6 pillowcases, one pair curtains and valences, half a dozen napkins, 2 table cloths, 2 chests, 3 old coffers, one trunk, 3 small boxes, one small joined stool, one chair, a press, one tack, one pewter platter and some other old lumber   £8 5s

Chamber over the Kitchen

One truckle bedstead and mat, one old bed and some old bedding, one table board, 6 planks, 2 old coffers, 3 small old barrels, one old half headed bedstead took a broad , 5 boards and some old timber, an old silt and a cheese rack, 2 small turns and an old reel with some other old implements   £2 5s

Total   £20   19s

BAKERS

Thomas Clement   **Baker**   **1635**   **P2/C/441**

Parlour

One table board with a frame, 2 coffers one standing bedstead and 2 joined stools   16s

One coverlet, one blanket, 2 bolsters, 2 pillows   £1

Hall

One table board with a joined frame, one cupboard, one form and 2 chairs   16s

One pair of iron tongs, one fire pan, 2 iron hangells, 2 broaches, one dripping pan, one powdering tub with other small things   8s

Buttery

One alembic, one warming pan, 3 little kettles, 3 crocks, 2 skillets, one pair of pothooks, one barrel, one brass pan, one powdering tub with other small things £2 6s

Half a dozen of pewter vessels and one basin 6s 8d

One other basin and one ewer, 2 candlesticks, one spice mortar, one salt, one pewter pot and one Bible 8s

Chamber over the Parlour

One little low bedstead, one old bed, one coverlet, one blanket and one bolster 9s

Chamber over the Shop

2 bedsteads, one cupboard with a press, 2 chests, one coffer, one little square table board with a frame £2 10s

One old flock bed, one flock bolster, 2 coverlets, one blanket, 3 pillows and one old carpet £1 6s 8d

9 large platters, 2 candlesticks, one salt, half a dozen of small pewter vessels with some other small things £1 3s 4d

Barton

3 load of logs and other small wood £1

Bunting House and Bakehouse

3 planks, 2 troughs, 3 tubs, one old witch and some other small things 10s

One old tub in the shop 1s

His wearing apparel £1 13s 4d

Of linen, 2 pairs of sheets, half a dozen napkins, one board cloth and 5 other, 6 small parcels of linen £1 8s

Total £16

Francis Yerbury senior   [Baker]   1676   P2/7/45

Chamber

One wainscot press	£1
6 leather chairs	15s
One trunk, 2 coffers, 4 joined stools	14s
One pair of brass andirons, one warming pan, one dresser, one pair of iron andirons	9s
2 bedsteads with 2 mats and cords	£1
2 feather beds, 2 feather pillows, one feather bolster	£4
2 flock beds, 3 bolsters, 2 pillows	£2
2 rugs, one old coverlet, 3 old blankets	£1 10s
One pair of curtains and valences	5s
5 napkins, 2 towels, one table cloth	5s
5 sheets, 5 pillow cases, 2 bolster cases	£1
One looking glass, one flasket and other small implements	1s

Lower Room

11 pewter platters	£2
3 flagons, 3 candlesticks, 4 pewter dishes, 2 pint tankards, one pewter bowl, one pewter chamber pot	14s
2 bell metal pots, one bell metal posnet, one brass pan, one kettle, one little kettle, one brass kettle pot with other small pieces	£1 15s
One iron roaster, 2 spits, 2 fire pans, one fire pick, one fire tongs, one pair of dogs, one pair of andirons, one pair of hangells, one twy crook, one pothook, one pair of bellows	15s
One table board, one form, one carpet, one joined chair, 2 rush bottom chairs, one cushion, one cupboard, 4 glasses, one half bushel with some other implements of earth	10s

Buttery

One plank, 4 barrels, one form, one joined safe, one powdering tub, one pail, one dough tub, one brewing tub, 2 little horses, 2 low stools, 3 small pieces of latten with some other small implements	£1 2s

Bakehouse

Utensils of trade	£1
2 table boards, one bedstead and other good all in the possession of Francis Yerbury junior	£1 5s

The executor half year	£4 15s
2 bonds	£15

Total   £41 15s

William Orpen   Baker   1700   P2/O/69

His wearing apparel — £3

Best Chamber

One flock bed and a bedstead with the furniture — £1 10s

One table board and frame, one chest, one coffer, 6 chairs — 18s 6d

Little Chamber

2 beds and bedsteads with the furniture — 15s 6d

One coffer — 9d

Lower Room

One kettle, two brass crocks, one skillet, one warming pan, 2 brass candle sticks — £1 1s

5 pewter platters and 4 plates, one tankard — 11s 3d

One pair of andirons, one frying pan, one pair tongs — 3s 6d

One little table board and frame, two joined stools, one cupboard, one set of peter shelves — 9s 4d

Bakehouse

One broach and some baking implements — 7s 4d

Wood Barton

2 load of faggots — £1 1s

One mare — £3

Lumber goods and things forgotten and unseen — 13s 4d

Some small book debts being desperate — £2 8s 3d

Total   £15 19s 9d

BUTCHER

Robert Fuller   Butcher   **1600   P2/F/55**

Hall
One round table board, 2 benches,one joined chair, one little joined stool,
   one trendle, 3 pair of hangells, one pair of pothooks   4s

Parlour
One table board with a frame, 2 benches, 2 joined stools, one joined bedstead
   and settle for the same, one joined cupboard   £1   13s   4d

Buttery
One horse to set drink on, 5 barrels, 2 cowls, one old barrel, one trendle,
   one pail, 3 dishes   5s
2 crocks, 2 skillets, one brass pan, 2 cauldrons   18s
2 platters, 2 pottingers, 2 saucers, one basin   4s
One broach, one dripping pan, one gridiron   1s   4d

Chamber over the Hall
One press, one coffer, one plank   5s
All his wearing apparel   £1
One pair of sheets, 2 board cloths, 2 pillow cases   12s
One dough trendle, one powdering, one kive, one old bedstead, one malt
   sieve   3s   8d

Little Chamber
One table board with a frame, one chest, one old cupboard, 2 benches, one
   little joined stool, 2 candlesticks, one stone cup, one salt, one cupboard
   cloth   10s

Chamber over the Little Chamber
One bedstead with a stained tester, one flock bed, one bolster, 2 blankets,
   2 coverlets, 2 feather pillows   £1
One little bedstead, 4 blankets, 2 pillows, 2 coverlets   6s   8d
One little coffer, one table board, 2 trestles, one flasket   2s

Shop

2 stocks, 2 rails with hooks, one cutting board	3s 4d
All the tools of his trade	5s

Barton

One pig, 2 troughs	5s
Half a load of wood	2s

Total   £8   0s   4d

WIDOWS AND SPINSTERS

Ann Box   Widow and weaver   1592   P2/B/142

Shop

Two broad looms with all the tackling	£2 10s

Hall

One table board, one pair of trestles, one form	1s 4d
One cupboard	3s
One form, 3 stools, one pail	6d
8 lbs of lead	4d
One hangell, one pair of pothooks, 2 brandirons, one pair of bellows, one iron shoe horn	1s 8d

Upper Chamber

One little table board, one cowl and 3 barrels	3s 6d
One horse to set drink on, one pail, one powdering tub, one kype, one board	3s 4d
One crock, one cauldron	5s
2 cauldrons, one frying pan, one chaffing dish	3s
One weigh beam and scales, one tun dish, one cup, one ring	8d
3 platters, 3 pottingers	6s
One basket, one stean, one malt sieve	8d
2 boards, 2 coffers, one little tack	3s 4d
One lye stone	4d
Half a dozen trenchers, half a dozen dishes, half a dozen spoons	6d

Inner Chamber

One bedstead, one stained cloth and one board	2s 8d
3 kivers, one malt sieve, one cowl, one plank board, one tack, one little board	3s 6d
One feather bed	10s
2 bedsteads, one flock bed	6s 8d
One flock bed	6s 8d
One reel and old board	6d
One weigh beam and scales, one kype	1s 8d
2 candlesticks of brass	1s
3 coverlets	£1
4 blankets	5s
One feather bolster and 2 flock bolsters	4s 8d
2 pillows of flock	2s
3 pairs of canvas sheets and one board cloth	£1 4s
2 pillows of holland	3s 4d
6 partlets and 3 bonds	5s
2 kerchiefs of holland and 4 of lockram	5s 4d
3 aprons of canvas, 3 of woollen and one of worsted	2s 8d
2 napkins, one waistcoat and 2 pairs of hand cuffs	1s 2d
2 smocks	2s
4 petticoats and one waistcoat	15s 4d
2 gowns of friese and one old gown	14s
2 waistcoats and hose and shoes	1s 4d
3 load of wood	10s
2 vats, 2 old kypes, one spinning turn, one little scarme and one lantern	2s 6d
One coverlet and one blanket	6s
One felt hat	2s
One waistcoat	6d
One bill, one pair of shoes, one salt cellar, one peck, one tankard	2s 2d

Total   £12   10s   2d

Elizabeth Bapshin   **Widow**   **1592**   **P2/B/139**

Hall

One table board, 2 trestles, one form	1s 4d
2 brandirons, 2 hangells, one pair of bellows, one pair of andirons, 3 broaches, 2 dripping pans, one gridiron	10s

Parlour

2 brass pans and 4 brass pots	£2 14s
3 pails, one cowl, 4 barrels, one silt	4s
One cupboard, one square table, one turn	3s 4d
One bedstead, one flock bed, two blankets	6s

Little Chamber

One bedstead, one flock bed, one tester, 2 blankets, one coverlet, one form	13s

Chamber over the Hall

2 bedstead, one flock bed, 2 bolsters, 3 coverlets, one pair of blankets, 2 pillows	£1 8s
One gown, 2 petticoats, 2 coffers	12s

New Loft

21 cheeses	7s
3 earthen pans, 2 earthen crocks	6d
11 crates of onions	1s
22 bushels of barley	£1 9s 4d
4 brass candlesticks and one of pewter	2s 6d
6 old platters, one brass basin, one salt	7s 8d
Old iron	2s
12 pounds of wool	6s
2 bushels of wheat	4s
One old bunting witch, one bushel, one peck, 2 old barrels, 2 old kypes	2s
2 shelves, one hatchet, one bill	2s
One weigh beam, one dung pick, one hand hook	1s
One wood hook and one nipper	8d
2 sacks and one wool sheet	2s

One bottle and 2 sieves	1s 4d
One board, one trestle and one cheese rack	4d

Blind Loft

One pack saddle, one girth, one pick, 2 old witches	3s

Barn

The corn in the barn	£7
One rick of barley and hay in the barton	£4 6s 8d
2 rick staddles	2s
The hay in the hay house	£4
One yetting trough	2s

Plough Harness

One iron bound wain	£3
One sullow, one drag and the aies	6s 8d
3 plough ropes, 2 yokes and bows	6s 8d

Cattle

17 sheep	£4
4 calves	£1 4s
4 oxen	£8
3 kine	£5
3 young beasts	£2
One mare and colt	£1 12s 8d
4 pigs	12s

Poultry

6 geese	3s
20 hens, pullets and cocks	5s

Corn and pasture in the field	
18 acres of wheat	£10
The herbage of the grounds	£1

Total   £63 6s 10d

Christian Phillips   **Widow**   **1592**   **P2/P/91**

Loft over the parlour

2 little table boards and one form	2s
2 board bedsteads	1s 8d
4 coffers	(--)
One press and small old boards	1s 4d
One trendle, 4 sieves, one reel and one earthen crutch	1s
One sack and one basket	4d

Parlour

2 little brass pots, 2 cauldrons, one pappron, 2 pans and one little skillet	14s
2 candlesticks, one chaffing dish, one skimmer	1s
2 frying pans, one pair of pothooks, 2 pair of hangells and one gridiron	3s 4d
2 stone cups, half a dozen spoons, 8 wooden dishes, one dozen trenchers	1s
5 earthen pots and 3 treen platters	6d
2 chairs, 2 stools, one joined form	6d
One bottle, one peck, one mouse snare, one lantern	10d
5 coverlets and one blanket	12s
One flock bed, 2 bolsters, 4 pillows	14s
2 pair of sheets, 2 pillow cases	12s
One towel, one board cloth, 4 aprons, 7 kerchiefs, 4 partlets, 4 napkins, 2 linen cloths	14s
Her wearing apparel	£1
3 stained cloths and one brush	1s 4d
4 cushions and one turn	1s 8d

In wood	4s

Total   £5 17s 4d

Parlour
One bedstead, one feather bed, one feather bolster, one coverlet, one pair of
blankets, one chest, one chair, one joined cupboard, one table board, one
form   £4 15s

High Chamber
One great brass pot, 6 brass pans, 2 small brass pots with divers other
implements   £5 6s 8d

Lower House
One malt quern, 2 hogsheads, one yetting stone and divers other implements   £1 14s

Buttery
One sieve, one brass pan, one small table board, a form, a pair of tables with
other Implements   13s 4d

Kitchen
3 brass pots, 3 spits, one furnace, 2 pair of andirons, one iron plate, 3 pair of
pothooks, 2 pair of iron hangells, one iron pitching bar, one table board, 2
chairs with other Implements   £5 3s 4d
One musket   10s

Malting Room
One bedstead and other implements   6s 8d

White House
3 vats, a cheese ring   5s

One other Upper Chamber
One bedstead, one feather bed, 2 bolsters, one canvas bed case, 5 feather
pillows 8 cushions, 2 carpets, 2 coverlets, 2 rugs, one joined press, 4 chests,
one warming pan, one pair of bellows, a fire tongs and a stool   £10 2s 4d
Linen   £2
Her wearing apparel   £10

Inner Chamber

One bedstead, 2 flock beds, 3 coverlets, 2 bolsters, one alembic, one spice
mortar, one chest with other implements   £2 5s
Pewter: one dozen and a half of platters, 6 pottingers, 6 saucers, 5 candle
sticks, one chaffing dish and a chamber pot   £1 10s

One wain, 3 yokes, 2 iron ropes, one drag, one pair of aies, one sullow,
2 rick staddles, one yetting stone, 2 ladders and one grab mill   £3

One silver bowl and 5 silver spoons which as yet are not come into the
possession of the executors   £2 5s

Total   £49 12s 8d

Elizabeth Howell	**Widow**	**1613**	**P1/H/75**

Hall

One table board, one form, one bench   2s 6d
One cupboard, 2 chairs, one stool   10s

Buttery

One brewing tub, one old brewing vat, one kive   3s 4d
4 barrels   4s
5 brass pans, one cauldron   £2
3 brass crocks, 2 brass skillets   13s 4d
2 sieves, one search, 2 rings   1s 6d
One bushel and one peck   1s 6d
6 wooden dishes, 2 bowls, 2 stone cups, one dozen and a half of trenchers,
3 tin spoons   12s
One horse for beer, one old form, one old board, 3 pitchforks, one black bill
2s

Kitchen

One table board, 2 forms, 2 tacks, one plank   4s
4 cheese vats, 2 salt tubs, one board and 2 trestles, one little salt stone   2s
One frying pan, 2 pothooks, 2 pothangers, 2 broaches, one brandiron,
one pair of iron dogs, one pair of tongs, one little iron bar   8s

Malt Loft

One witch for corn	2s 6d
6 bushels of wheat	£1 4s
One trundle bedstead	1s 6d
2 pairs of scales	1s
4 leaden weights	1s 8d
One old butter basket, one spinning wheel. 2 pieces of old wool cards and 6 old boards	4s
One little oatmeal tub, one old reel, 3 pounds of old iron	8d

Garden

One cheese ring, one yetting stone, to the well one bucket and one rope	10s
2 dozen of helm	3s
2 loads of wood	10s
The fruit of the garden	5s

Chamber over the Buttery

2 standing bedsteads	£1 6s
2 flock beds and one bolster, 3 pillows	£1
3 pairs of sheets	£1
2 coverlets, one pair of blankets	£1
2 towels	3s 4d
2 board cloths	2s 6d
2 pillows	3s
One table napkin	6d
5 smocks	6s 10d
6 aprons	6s
9 partlets	10s
8 kerchiefs	6s
One fustian waistcoat	1s
One cloth gown of mingle colour	£1
One stamel petticoat	16s
2 old cloth gowns	10s
3 old cloth petticoats	6s 8d
6 pounds of wool	6s
One swath band	4d
3 silver spoons	10s

2 silver rings	3s
One old hat and a band to it	1s
2 pairs of shoes, 2 pairs of stockings	4s
One wainscot chest	6s 8d
2 coffers	6s 8d
2 old cushions	6d
2 books	2s
2 little brass candlesticks	1s 6d

Chamber over the Hall

One field bedstead	3s 4d
One flock bed and one bolster	6s 8d
2 coverlets, one pair of blankets	10s
One cheese rack	6d

Little Buttery

One pewter bottle	1s
One kiver, one grater	6d
2 trestles	6d
2 pounds of blue wool	2s

Corn and grass in the field

4 acres of wheat	£2
3 acres of barley	£1 19s
A backside containing one acre	10s
One half acre lanes end	5s
The rent of the house beyond the bridge	£1 8s
4 couples of sheep	£1
3 wether sheep	12s
Without the door, a stone trough	4d
One old tree in the backside beyond the bridge	1s 6d

Total   £27 18s 10d

Elizabeth Taunton alias Bayly   (Leigh)   1663   P2/T/227

Parlour

One standing bedstead	£1 10s
One drawing table board	10s
4 high joined stools	2s
One livery table	6s 8d
One joined chair, one triggen chair	3s 4d
One great leather chair	2s 6d
One low back stool	6d
One feather bed and bolster, curtains and valences, cord and mat	£2
Andirons, one pair fire shovels and tongs with brass head	3s
4 wrought cushions	6s
One green cupboard cloth	4s
One arras carpet cloth	4s
One felt quilt	£1 10s

Hall

One long table board, one carpet thereto belonging, 8 tufted cushions, 6 joined stools	£1 4s
One plain table with a carpet, 2 forms	12s
2 great joined chairs	4s
One little square table with a carpet thereto belonging	3s 4d
One cupboard with drawers	10s
One cushion thereon	2s 6d
2 rush chairs	1s
One pair of iron andirons	3s 4d

Kitchen

One high joined chair, 2 short forms	1s 6d
One great brass pot	£2
2 brass pots and one posnet	£1 10s
3 brass cast skillets	4s
One skillet in his frame	1s 4d
One brass chaffing dish, one warming pan, one brass kettle, one brass ladle, 2 skimmers	7s
3 brass candlesticks	10s

5 brass pans	£2
One copper kettle	13s 4d
One other brass kettle	3s
5 broaches, 2 iron dripping pans, 2 gridirons, 4 pothooks	5s
One pair of iron racks	6s 8d
One pair of iron dogs	3s 4d
One firepan and tongs	3s
One jack to turn broach	6s 8d
One dozen and one of pewter plates, great and small	£1
2 great pewter plates to set under pies and 2 little ones, one little basin, 4 saucers, one salt and one pewter candlestick	4s
2 flagons, 2 pewter pots	8s
2 pewter custard pans, 2 chamber pots and a latten colander	2s
One iron chaffing dish	6d
One frying pan	1s 6d

White House

One cheese press	4s
9 barrels	10s
2 cowls	5s
One butter churn	1s 6d
2 leather bottles	1s 2d
One tenon saw	6d

Old Kitchen

One long trendle, 4 round trendles, one kive and one measuring vat	12s
2 brandirons	8d
One old horse to set barrels on	4d
One ring, one search, one peck	2s

Hall Chamber

One bedstead, curtain and valence, cord and mat with a flock bed thereon	£1 6s 8d
One other flock bed with his appurtenances	12s
One spruce chest	£1
2 other chests and a joined chair and a little box with drawers	14s 6d
One arras coverlet	12s

One other coverlet branched green colour   10s
One boarden standing press   1s 6d
One trundle bedstead, cord and mat   4s
One feather bed, 2 feather bolsters   £1 10s

Parlour Chamber
One livery bedstead with a flock bed, rug, blankets, bolster with a settle   £1 6s 8d

Chamber over the Kitchen
One standing bedstead, one feather bed with a bolster, coverlet and blankets   10s
One standing stool   6d

Cockloft
One old coverlet and blanket   1s

More in the Hall
One basin and ewer   6s 8d
2 sconces for candles, one pair of samplers   1s 6d
Diverse other small pieces in the several rooms of household stuff   2s 6d
Plate: 2 silver salts, one bowl, one suble, one cup, 4 silver spoons   £6

Cattle and plough harness
3 yoke of oxen   £24
5 cows and 2 heifers   £15
2 weanling calves   £1
5 pigs   £1 6s 8d
20 loads of hay   £18
Corn in the barn and in rick   £16
Plough harness, one wain bed, one dung pot, one drag, 3 aies, 2 pair of wheels, 5 iron ropes, 3 yokes, 2 sullows, 2 shares and 2 coulters   £2 10s

Total   £118 15s 10d

Elizabeth Beaman   Widow   1679   P2/B/951

Hall

16 small pieces of pewter and 16 larger, one chamber pot, one flagon, one
tankard, one pair of brass candlestick, 1 pair latten, one dozen spoons, 2
brass pans, 3 skillets, 5 brass crocks, one brass chaffing dish, 3 old kettles
£5   13s 4d

2 spits, one pair andirons, one pair dogs, one fire pan and tongs, a
cleaver and randing knife, a steel box, an iron standard, a mustard bowl,
2 pair hangells, a bacon rack, a basting ladle, one pair of bellows, 2 old
Bibles, with other small implements, one table board, 3 forms, one joined
stool, one old settle, 3 chairs, 2 old stools and shelves and dresser
£2 3s 4d

Buttery

4 old barrels, one old cupboard, a horse for to set beer, 3 shelves, one dozen
trenchers, a powdering tub, a search with other small implements   13s 8d

Mill Chamber

5 old tubs, 2 pails, one stock of wood and coal, one old flock bed with some
old bedding and some other old implements   £3 3s 4d

Backside

One breeding pig with pig troughs   £1 6s 8d

Cockloft

Board and other lumber   £1

Chamber over the Hall

3 flock beds, 4 pair of sheets, 3 pair blankets and 2 bolsters and two cases,
3 pillows and 3 cases, one rug, and one coverlet, one tester bedstead, one
other old bedstead, a truckle bedstead, one chest, 2 old coffers, one joined
chair, half a dozen napkins, one old table cloth, one holland sheet, half a
dozen holland and dowlas pillow cases with some other small implements
£8 2s 8d

In money and desperate debts   £5
A silver spoon and old gold ring   £1 5s 8d
Her wearing apparel both linen and woollen   £5

Total   £33 12s 8d

Elizabeth King   **Widow**   **1687**   **P2/K/253**

Wearing apparel: one black gown, 3 petticoats, one great chest with a lock,
   one box, one Bible, one looking glass with some part of her linen   £3
One tester bedstead, cord and mat   12s
One tuck feather bed, 2 pillows   £2 10s
One red rug   10s
One feather bed, one green rug, one flock bolster and 2 pairs of blankets   £2
One bedstead with a buckram covering, cord and mat and iron rods   10s
One set of curtains and valences   12s
2 coverlets   3s
One great chest, 2 coffers, 3 boxes, 2 chairs   18s 6d
One leather painted cushion and other things   2s
4 dowlas sheets, one dozen dowlas napkins, one board cloth   £1 12s
3 bolster cases, 4 pillow cases, one old bed case, one little board cloth   8s
One great cupboard, one little cupboard, one table board, one old joined stool
   16s

One brass pan, one great kettle, one little kettle, one brass pot, 3 bell metal
   pots, one posnet, mortar and pestle, one skillet   £1 12s
One warming pan, one skimmer   1s 6d
2 flagons, 7 pewter platters, one plate and 2 saucers   18s
A pair of andirons, one pair of dogs and fender, fire pan and tongs,
   2 hangells, 2 spits, one box iron and frying pan, one iron dripping pan
   £1 2s
3 old latten pans, 2 iron candlesticks   1s
One wooden bottle, 2 washing tubs, 2 kivers, 4 barrels, one powdering tub,
   one pail, wooden horse   £1 1s
One leather bag and 2 chairs   2s
A sack of feathers, a small parcel of wool, one plank, 2 shelves   4s
2 dozen and 10 trenchers   2s
2 locks and some old iron   3s

Bad debts abroad   £5

Total   £24

OCCUPATIONS NOT GIVEN

Richard Rundle snr   **1576**   **P2/R/11**

One cupboard and 2 andirons	8s
2 pothangers and a fire tongs	1s
2 forms and a round table board	3s 2d
2 joined forms	2s 8d
A long table board, a long form and 2 trestles	3s 4d
2 coffers	2s 8d
One white tester, 2 white coverlets and one old coverlet	7s
One flock bed, one bolster and 2 pillows	9s 8d
One pair of new blankets	6s 8d
2 old carpets	3s 4d
A truckle bedstead and 2 chairs	1s 8d
His wearing apparel	8s 4d
One pair of holland sheets and 2 pairs of other sheets	16s
4 old green cloths hanging about the house	1s
8 platters, 2 pottingers, one saucer, 3 candlesticks	12s
3 little brass pans and a skillet	10s
3 cauldrons and a paperne	7s 6d
One frying pan and a dripping pan	2s
One crock and a broach	4s
One short table, 2 stools, 2 tacks, 2 bottles	1s
2 sanges and a weigh beam	1s 4d
12 inch boards	2s
One broad board	2s 6d

Total   £6   1s

Nicholas Willis **1593** **P2/W/100**

Hall
2 table boards, 2 forms, 2 benches 3s

Chamber
In money 10s
2 flock beds, 2 coverlets, one bolster, one pair of blankets, one cloak £1
6 coffers 10s
2 cupboards 3s
2 sheets and 2 shirts 10s

3 cauldrons 4s
2 brass pans and one skillet 3s
6 brass pots and one pair of pothooks £1
4 platters, 7 pottingers, one saucer, 2 salt cellars, 4 candlesticks 6s

One wooden beam and scales and 20 pounds of lead 1s 8d
2 frying pans, one broach, one brass chaffing dish, one grid iron,
  one brand iron, one hangell, one fire pan 2s 6d

2 black bills 1s 8d
2 barrels, one meal bowl, 2 pails, 2 kivers 2s

2 bedsteads 10d
His wearing apparel 8s

2 shovels, one hedging bill, 3 ladders, one stone hammer, one trowel 3s 4d
One iron bar, 8 wedges 3s
All his tools 13s 4d
4 spinning turns 4s

Total £6 19s 4d

Simon Daniell   **1630**   **P2/D/160**

Hall

One chair	2s 6d
One spinning turn	8d
3 boards, a tack and a form	1s 2d
3 barrels, one tub, 2 pails, one horse for beer	4s
2 dough trendles	1s
A wooden platter	2d
A peppercorn, a wooden candlestick	2d
A basin	1s 6d
A spit, a chopping knife, 2 twy crocks	1s

Chamber

One feather bed, one bolster, one coverlet, one blanket	£1 15s
2 coffers, 2 bedsteads	5s
A tallet, a reel, a ring, a malt sieve	2s 6d
His wearing apparel	£1 10s
His working tools	9s
His wood and a ladder	14s 8d

Total   £5 9s 10d

These goods following were in the house but were the goods of his wife being a widow when he married her and the property never altered.

One table board, one form, 3 stools	3s
12 old dishes, one form, 3 stools	1s 8d
A drinking cup and a can	2d
2 brass pans	£1
3 brass pots	13s 6d
A skillet, a skimmer, 12 spoons	2s 6d
A pair of hangells, a flesh hook, a pair of pothooks	1s
10 pewter dishes and 3 saucers	13s 4d
2 pewter candlesticks and 2 brass candlesticks, a pewter beaker and a salt	5s
2 flock beds, 4 bolsters, 2 pillows, one carpet, 3 coverlets, 2 blankets, 2 pairs of sheets	£3 15s
One coffer	2s

Total   £6 17s 2d

Glossary

abb	weft yarn
aies	light harrows
alembic	distilling apparatus
andiron	iron bar to support the end of a log in a fire
arras carpet cloth	tapestry wallhanging
beckhorn	anvil with points at each end
birdng piece	gun for shooting birds
boytling stocks	possibly a bottle rack
broach	the rod of a spit
bubbing board	board to dress cloth by removing bumps
bucking cowl	steeping bowl
buckram	coarse or stiff cloth
cadiz	type of woollen cloth
camleat	type of cloth
chaffing dish	container for food to be placed under a brazier
clift	wood cut up for fuel
cowl	cask in which malt liquor cools
crutch	large bowl
culver	type of gun
diaper	linen cloth
dornick	cloth from Doornick a Flemish town
dowlas	coarse linen cloth
dung pot	strong cart for carrying manure
felloes	curved outer sections of a wooden wheel
flock bed	mattress filled with waste wool
fustian	coarse, twilled cloth
golom	galloon, narrow ribbon for trimming clothes
graffing saw	saw for grafting
Hamborough cloth	cloth from Hamborough (Germany)
hamses	part of the collar of a draught horse

132

hangells	iron rod over a fire, for pots to hang on and with teeth so that it could be moved up and down
helm	straw
hogshead	a large cask of varying quantity
holland cloth	cloth from the Low Countries
horse for beer	wooden frame for holding barrels
inkle	tape
jemells	type of hinge
kadell cup	caudle cup for gruel
kersey	coarse woollen cloth
kilderkin	a cask holding 16 to 18 gallons
kipe	basket
kiver	shallow wooden vessel
latten basin	basin of metal like pewter
linsey wolsey	inferior cloth made of wool and flax
list wool	selvedge
lockram	coarse linen cloth
mangfodder	possibly an animal foodstuff made with mangels
mat and cord	cloth covering the cords across the base of a bedstead
metheglin	a spiced form of mead
pannel	a kind of saddle
paperne/pappron	dish for keeping food warm
partlet	piece of clothing worn by women around the neck and chest
pease	pulse
peck	container holding 2 gallons
plocks	blocks of sawn wood
Pope's minister	type of cloth
posnet	small metal vessel with 3 feet
pothook	rod for holding pots over the fire

pottinger	dish for holding soup, etc
pottle pot	a pot with a capacity of about half a gallon
powdering tub	tub for salting
press engine	press used by clothworkers and perhaps in other processes
pritchell	pointed tool for making holes
quern	stones for grinding corn
quilling turn	implement for making pleats
randing knife	knife for trimming leather
rene	leather measurement
ring	implement used in cheese making
rudder beast	ox kept for fattening
rundire/runlet	small cask
scarme/scirme	a baton for consolidating the weft in weaving
sasnet	sarcenet, a kind of thin cloth used for linings
scrafe	slatted stand for keeping cloth off the floor when fulling
seedlip	implement for broadcasting seed
serge	hard wearing woollen cloth
serpler	large sack in which wool was delivered
silt	trough for salting meat
staddle	stone pillar for raising haystacks and granaries off the ground
stadges	desk on which cloth was put when raising the nap with teasels
stamel	coarse woollen cloth used for undergarments, usually red
standard	a frame to support a table board
stean	earthenware vessel with 2 handles
steeling iron	sharpening steel
strike	stick for levelling off measures of grain
sullow	plough
swatchband	sample piece of cloth

tallet	a loft
tester	bed with canopy over
tick	hard linen material
treen	utensils made of wood
trencher	wooden dish
trendle	tub for making dough
triggen chair	wickerwork chair
truckle bed	bed which fits under the main bed
tun dish	shallow vessel with a hole used as a funnel
turn	spinning wheel
wain	waggon
weigh beam	steelyard scale
wether sheep	castrated male sheep
whipples	part of plough harness
wimble	gimlet
winnower	implement for separating the wheat from the chaff
witch	bin made of planks
yetting stone	stone, possibly a trough, used in steeping barley in malting

Words and objects whose meaning is unknown or uncertain:

bascrell; boone; crocus; fell wool; forret; furnitude; Hastan cloth; keeps; moudges; neast hurdle; plash; prisons; raying sieve; sanges; sistells; suble; twig; whisker

Index of names